Read this book for the sake of sharing the Good News with Cultural Chinese! I'Ching Thomas, has aptly pointed out that the reception of the Christian religion by Cultural Chinese has never been an easy path ever since Christianity reached the shores of China more than ten centuries ago. With exceptional clarity, I'Ching identifies the core belief of the Cultural Chinese as the belief in human flourishing based on Confucianism. Without undermining the contribution of Confucius to humanity, I'Ching presents the biblical belief of human flourishing as the state of *shalom*, in which God restores humanity from its fallen predicament through the redemptive work of His only begotten Son Jesus Christ.

Rev Dr Clement Mook-Soo Chia
Principal
Singapore Bible College

Jesus: The Path to Human Flourishing does us an enormous service. China is expanding its vision as a global citizen and its people are increasingly settling throughout the world. Those of us who love the gospel of Christ and love all things Chinese — and I am certainly one — have been desperate for a single volume that can expertly guide us through the rich moral and spiritual history of Chinese thought, and then show us how the story of Scripture, from Creation, to Fall, to the ultimate harmony of God's kingdom, both challenges and fulfils the longings of the Chinese heart. As someone serving in a city, and a local church, blessed with a growing Chinese population, I am very grateful to I'Ching Thomas for the years of work evident in this book.

Rev Dr John Dickson (Ph.D.)
Author, historian, Founding Director of the Centre for Public Christianity,
and Rector of St Andrew's Roseville (Sydney)

I0521895

In an era when China's political leaders and intellectual elites are doubling down on their criticism of Christianity as a "foreign" religion, I'Ching Thomas's book provides a timely response to the age-old question of how the gospel relates to Chinese culture. Bringing together the Hebrew concept of *shalom* and the Chinese notion of the *junzi*, or Noble Man, she makes a strong argument for human flourishing as the common aspiration bridging the two traditions. Building on this common ground, she constructs an apologetic that speaks to the relational nature of Chinese culture, allowing for a meaningful dialog that engages the heart as well as the mind. For Chinese Christians struggling to share their faith with non-believing relatives, as well as for non-Chinese who seek to relate the truth of the Gospel within the Chinese worldview, this book provides a positive way forward.

Dr Brent Fulton
President and Founder
ChinaSource

This is a must-read book for anyone serious about building better evangelistic models for reaching more Cultural Chinese today. With great insight and clarity in so many areas, I'Ching Thomas tells us the history that led to why Chinese people actually think the way they do. More importantly, she provides new insights on how we can use that understanding to build better bridges with Cultural Chinese today. In writing this book, she provides a great service to the body of Christ in helping us better understand what may be missing in our approach to reaching more Chinese today. Most importantly, she shows us how God's work in human history actually provides the ideal blue print to fulfill the deep longings of the Chinese heart!

Dr David Geisler
President, Norm Geisler International Ministries
Adjunct Prof, Southern Evangelical Seminary

I'Ching Thomas has written something very important for those who wish to build bridges and not walls between world cultures. She has provided us a brilliant road map that has the real potential to heal an ages-old rift between traditional Chinese culture and the Christian West. Her project highlights the noble goals of Confucian thought for the betterment of humankind, but adds something that other writers and thinkers tend to leave out: a real source of power that can bring these traditional aspirations to a point of full flourishing. She offers a solution that is not imported from overseas, but one that comes from above, with power to achieve true peace for individuals and society, and to achieve the most noble ends.

Craig J. Hazen, Ph.D.
Director of Graduate Studies
Biola University

Eastern religions in China have often been described and discussed, but the transformative impact of the gospel in Chinese culture has received scant recognition. I'Ching Thomas's remarkable work reveals how one can meaningfully connect with the Cultural Chinese through our Christian faith without rejecting their history and culture. *Jesus: The Path to Human Flourishing* provides a clear and fascinating insight to engaging the Cultural Chinese with Scripture. This book is about building bridges, and embracing the world's largest and, perhaps, most energetic population.

Lawrence Tong
International Director
Operation Mobilisation

We cannot contextualize biblical truth without first understanding context. I'Ching Thomas helpfully identifies key points of intersection between Chinese culture and the gospel. Contextualization requires humility and earnest reflection. Thomas demonstrates both when discerning biblical concerns found in various Eastern traditions. While readers won't agree with her on every page, her book will certainly catalyze productive conversation.

Jackson Wu
Professor of Theology & Missiology
Themelios, M&C Book Reviews Editor
Jacksonwu.org

Jesus: The Path to Human Flourishing

THE GOSPEL FOR THE CULTURAL CHINESE

by I'Ching Thomas

And he said to them, "Follow me, and I will make you fishers of men."
— MATTHEW 4:19

Jesus: The Path to Human Flourishing
Copyright © 2018 I'Ching Chan-Thomas

Published by Graceworks Private Limited
22 Sin Ming Lane
#04-76 Midview City
Singapore 573969
Tel: 67523403
Email: enquiries@graceworks.com.sg
Website: www.graceworks.com.sg

All Scripture quotations, unless otherwise indicated, are taken from *The Holy Bible, English Standard Version*. Copyright © 2000; 2001 by Crossway Bibles, a division of Good News Publishers. Used by permission. All rights reserved.

Design by Intent Design & Consultancy Pte Ltd

ISBN: 978-981-11-5718-9

3 4 5 6 7 8 9 10 • 25 24 23 22 21 20 19

For my family,
that spans two great cultures.

Contents

xi   Foreword

1   CHAPTER 1
Introduction: Why You're Talking
But We're Not Hearing

13   CHAPTER 2
Rethinking the Good News

31   CHAPTER 3
Religion of the Way: Daoism

43   CHAPTER 4
Religion of the Learned: Confucianism

53   CHAPTER 5
Religion of Buddha

67   CHAPTER 6
Confucius's Utopia

79   CHAPTER 7
Yahweh's Shalom

93   CHAPTER 8
Jesus: The Noble Path to Human Flourishing

119   ENDNOTES

Foreword

Christianity has a message for all people. Unfortunately, in many cultures, particularly ones with other dominant religions, the people cannot see how the religion of the Bible would add anything to their lives. This barrier is particularly significant if their introduction to Christianity occurred via European imperialism and its concomitant exploitations. China is a good case in point, as I'Ching Thomas explains in her book.

My observation is that around the globe there are frequently two undesirable reactions when Christianity is presented to people without concern for their indigenous culture. One is that the people consider Christianity to be an alien, Western religion and restrict its practice, maybe even prohibit it. The other surprisingly common reaction has been that the newly reached cultures find some way of "colonizing" Christianity. By that I mean that the people of those cultures not only accept Christianity, but syncretize it with their already existent beliefs to the point that they claim a privileged standing before God, ahead of any other nations and cultures, an attitude that is surely incompatible with biblical teaching. Again, we can see both of these extreme perspectives coming out of various pockets of Chinese culture today.

Without creating forced connections, I'Ching Thomas shows us that, despite the obstacles, Christianity is clearly appropriate for the Chinese people as much as for anyone else. Ancient Chinese philosophies and religions (specifically, Confucianism, Daoism, and Chinese Buddhism) hold up high ideals. They provide concepts and practices that should be of great benefit to their adherents in this life and for eternity. Even when we realize that the traditions per se cannot fulfill their promises, the ideals are not lessened; they just appear unattainable.

However, writing from her own experience and an impressive amount of scholarship, Thomas shows that Jesus, in his person and through his work, when rightly understood, directly addresses and fulfills the goals that have evaded the ancient sages.

This book exudes fairness on the intellectual level and usefulness on the practical side. It is very readable and makes a valuable contribution for anyone engaged in presenting the Christian gospel in the context of Chinese culture.

Winfried Corduan, PhD
Professor Emeritus of Philosophy and Religion
Taylor University

Author of Neighboring Faiths *and* In the Beginning God: A Fresh Look at the Case for Original Monotheism

Jesus: The Path to Human Flourishing

CHAPTER 1

Introduction: Why You're Talking But We're Not Hearing

The people may be made to follow a path of action, but they may not be made to understand it.

Kongzi

I have a confession — I can't swim. When I was merely five my mother decided to place me under the auspices of the Buddhist Goddess of Mercy, *Guanyin*. Apparently when I was dedicated to the Goddess over fire, a medium at the temple warned my mother that I should be kept away from large bodies of water as I was prone to death by drowning. Consequently, when I was at the prime age for swimming lessons, I was denied the opportunity and have never since had the chance to pick up the skill. Fortunately should a day come when I'm drowning, my son, who started learning swimming when he was four, promised that he would save me!

The driving force behind such superstitious beliefs in my family was my late maternal grandmother. My grandmother, before she passed on, was the empress of our family. *PohPoh's* petite and almost frail physique was most unfitting for her undeterred and strong will. Her domineering grip on her family was expected as she was a typical Hakka woman who survived the Japanese invasion in the 1940s as well as her husband's abandonment of her and their four young children when she was barely 30 years old. Her unsparing life had left her soul scarred, hardened, but no less determined to change her destiny.

At the same time, the tragic events of her life also led her to believe that all of life is fated — since her cards had been dealt, she would work with them and try to appease (and perhaps even manipulate) the heavens for a change in her luck. Hence, she was extremely superstitious — firmly committed to her religious beliefs, she was dutiful in her allegiance to the variety of gods at her favorite temple. However, during the last years of her life, she decided to start attending a church as she was distressedly concerned that her only son, who had become a Christian decades before, would not give her a proper send-off when her time on earth was up. She reckoned that if she became a Christian he would not hesitate to participate in her funeral rites as any filial son would and should.[1]

Uncle Alfred (*PohPoh's* only son) became a follower of Jesus when he was a teenager. His conversion was nothing less than a miracle considering the circumstances around it — single-mother family living in a Chinese new village of a small town in Malaysia. These "new villages" were really suburbs created by the British colonialists in the 1950s to prevent the Communist resurgence from spreading among ethnic Chinese in Malaya. As such these New Villages were mostly populated by ethnic

Chinese and hence very Chinese socially and culturally. Nonetheless, despite living in such a decidedly Chinese environment, Uncle Alfred became a Christian and started attending a Cantonese Baptist church in the village. His conversion marked the beginning of the Lord's work in my maternal family as, along with him, his youngest sister started attending church.

I was the third on my mother's side of the family to have become a follower of Jesus. Growing up in the seventies' multi-ethnic and multi-religious Malaysia, we simply assumed that all religions are the same — they all teach us to be good or moral, they bring peace and order into one's life, etc. While we express our reverence in different ways, we are all ultimately relating to the same God or a God. My Muslim best friend may appear very pious as she prays five times a day, but I am equally religious as I offer joss stick incense three times a day to the idols on our household altar. My mother, though a regular visitor to the Daoist temple, did not hesitate to ask my uncle to bring me to Sunday School on occasion as she believed that they teach children good things in church.

However, when I was 15, overwhelmed by teenage angst, the daunting questions of life haunted me: Who am I? Where did I come from? Why am I here? Where is my life heading? I was seeking and longing for meaning and purpose. I wanted answers. This existential ache further intensified with the sudden and tragic death of my eight-year-old cousin. I was demoralized and felt that there really was no point in my living if there was no purpose for my existence! Then, as I was clearing up after doing my school homework, a tract I randomly picked up from the occasional Sunday School class I attended fell out from one of the books. It was based on Psalm 34:8: "*Oh, taste and see that the LORD is good! Blessed is the man who takes refuge in him!*"

Three years after that evening, when I made the commitment to follow Jesus, I prayed for boldness as I approached my mother to ask for her permission to be baptized in water. Her first question was, "Will you still be able to eat with us when we serve foods that have been offered to idols on the table?" After I assured her I would still be able to do so, she granted her consent. Twenty years later, I would have the privilege and joy to witness her baptism and, subsequently, her sister's after being born again by the grace of Jesus Christ.

If you are a Cultural Chinese[2] and a first-generation follower of Christ in your family, chances are you will have many stories that are very similar to mine. In fact, I can bet that my mother's foremost concern for my new-found faith — whether I would be able to eat with the family post-baptism — is not at all peculiar in view of the significance of communal meals in a Cultural Chinese household. In addition, you would also be able to identify with my family's value of maintaining the harmony of relationships, and life's ultimate goal of prosperity. Navigating what onlookers might call passive-aggression that characterizes the behavior of so many Cultural Chinese is merely a way of life for us.

A common question I encounter in my interaction with Cultural Chinese believers when I speak at churches (no matter in Singapore or in Berkeley, California) is how they can relevantly share with their loved ones that this man, who is from a foreign land and from a culture that is equally distant, is the Savior their heart is meant for. How is accepting the lordship of a foreign man who was shamefully executed as a criminal in a time past be good news to the Cultural Chinese who take pride in being one of the most self-sufficient people that ever lived. Think of our celebrated inventions: paper, printing, compass, gunpowder, and the ancient wisdom of Confucius and Laozi.

If you are not a Cultural Chinese, you may find the Cultural Chinese's social and cultural values rather alien and even odd. Think of the many times you have wondered why rituals and formalities are so crucial that they can make or break relationships. Or the frustration you experienced when you can almost never get a straight *No* from a Cultural Chinese.

A few years ago I found myself among a privileged few invited to train over 200 house church pastors from mainland China in apologetics. After I finished my presentation, a question was handed to me: "Why must we preach the message of a foreign Jesus when the ancient wisdom of Kongzi and Laozi has already revealed to us the Way (the Dao[3]) even long before Jesus was born?" While these were already believers in Jesus (and were serving as pastors!), they also genuinely had an issue with God revealing his salvific truth in a supposed Western setting.

Anyone who has ever interacted with Cultural Chinese on spiritual or religious matters, would have come across the objection that Christianity is a Western religion and hence unsuited for Asians. "Christianity is a religion for Westerners. We Asians have our own religions," they would insist. Unfortunately, access to the worldwide web and the economic success of China in the last decade have not changed this misperception — in Qufu, Shandong, the Christian church is still not allowed to build her own building and believers can only meet to worship in a temporary make-do shelter because of opposition from local Confucianists. Some Chinese even insist that they will not celebrate Christmas because they are Chinese.[4]

Christianity: A Western Cultural Invasion?

Since Christianity (or at least some form of it[5]) arrived on the shores of China in AD 635, it has been perceived as a foreign religion and hence irrelevant for the Cultural Chinese.[6] The *One more Christian, one fewer Chinese* chant on May 4, 1919, in China further reinforced and perpetuated the misconception that when one chooses to follow Jesus, one has denounced one's Chinese identity to go after a foreign or Western god and ideology. A Chinese commits a great offense against his ancestor and nation when he pledges allegiance to Jesus.

According to historian Wu Xiaoxin, the propaganda that impacted the Chinese the most is the claim that "*Religion is the opium of the people.*"[7] One of the main contributing factors to the hostile reaction to Christianity is nationalism. Anyone familiar with the events in this part of the world during the mid-1800s would realize the baggage this statement bears. Since the 19th century, Christianity has been associated with Western imperialism in the minds of Chinese people — both Catholics and Protestants came to China together with Western Imperialists.

In fact, many of the Western missionaries of that generation rode on the coattails of the European opium traders to bring the gospel to the Chinese.[8] For example, Karl Gutzlaff, an early Protestant missionary to China, joined the Jardine Matheson opium fleet as the interpreter in order to reach more Chinese with the gospel.[9]

Former Peking University president, Jiang Menglin, aptly described this historical baggage when he compared the arrival of Buddhism and Christianity in China: "Buddha rode into China on a white elephant, while Jesus rode in on a cannonball."[10] The anti-missionary feeling was understandable in view of the circumstances under which the modern missionary movement in China began: the same door that was forced open by military and naval power to expand trade was the door through which missionaries entered China. This compromised the gospel in Chinese eyes for the next century.

Although Christianity is not identical with Western Imperialism, they were both synonymous in the perception and memories of the Chinese. As a result, the encounter between Christianity and Chinese culture in the modern missionary era came with struggle between nationalism (and patriotism) and imperialism.[11] Even though personal relationships extended to deep friendships between Chinese and missionaries, in the background there always lingered the fact of missionaries being representatives of the foreign powers whose assault on China was all too obvious.[12]

As the Chinese saw their land endure one humiliation after another at the hands of foreigners in the nineteenth and early twentieth centuries, they came to regard Christianity as the representative of Western cultural imperialism. In addition, the gospel along with the beliefs it represents is entirely foreign to the Cultural Chinese worldview thus far and consequently some have considered the spread of Christianity as a kind of cultural invasion.

While it is undeniable that at some point in Chinese history Westerners who called themselves Christians were involved in oppressing and exploiting the Chinese, we need to differentiate Western imperialism and colonialism from Christianity. These Westerners did much harm to the Chinese but it must be recognized that many Western Christian missionaries also contributed greatly to the community where they worked in. Many sacrificed their lives to serve the Chinese people and built various institutions like schools, hospitals, orphanages and so on. For example, it must be remembered that during the tumultuous years of the second world war many Western missionaries and doctors stayed behind risking their lives to tend to and help the injured and dying.[13] And prior to the war, many Christian missionaries were instrumental in setting up schools and universities throughout Asia in the 1800's. Ubiquitous schools like the Anglo Chinese schools and Methodist colleges were all established by missionaries in the likes of James Legge, Robert Morrison and others.

Tu Weiming, the renowned modern-day Confucianist and a Sinologist, rightly applauds Christianity's contribution to China's intellectual landscape[14]:

While national universities, notably Peking, Nankai, Fudan, and Central, may have produced more political leaders, graduates from the Christian universities provided important human resources for virtually all professions. Furthermore, by emphasizing a liberal arts education, Christian universities trained several generations of modern scholars in the humanities and social sciences. Although all Christian universities were outlawed with the founding of the People's Republic, their alumni, numbering in the thousands, continued to play a vital role in many fields, including economics, diplomacy, education and journalism. Despite Zhou Enlai's critique of American cultural imperialism, the legacy of the Christian influence on Chinese higher education is indelible. ... After all, ever since the mid-nineteenth century, Christians have been champions of woman's liberation, medical care for the poor, human rights, and philanthropy.

The belief that Christianity is a Western or Westerners' religion is also far from being true as Christianity is a divine plan of salvation for all mankind regardless of heritage or ethnicity. In fact, to be historically accurate, the Christian faith had its early setting in the East rather than the West! Neither Jesus nor the Apostles were Westerners. Though as a result of historical development, Christianity did come to us from the West, it is a known fact that the Christian faith actually originated in Asia.

Being a Paul to the Cultural Chinese

Chinese Christian scholar, Xie Fuya, who spent most of his life analyzing the relationship between Christianity and Chinese culture believes the reason for the many misunderstandings and conflicts between the two is because Christianity has not yet comprehended Chinese culture. Consequently, Chinese culture does not fully fathom the essence of the faith while Christianity has not been able to impress and influence the Chinese culture.[15] Perhaps this is oversimplifying an issue that is much more complex, but I think in doing so Xie has actually stumbled upon something that is unique about the Christian faith.

Unlike the other foreign religion in China — Buddhism — Christianity is a canonical and exclusive religion. It makes exclusive truth claims about God and reality. However Buddhism is much more inclusive doctrinally. (This will be discussed at length later.) As such, it was able to assimilate congenially into the Cultural Chinese spirituality — accommodating and conforming to local philosophies which resulted in various indigenous permutations of the religion — affording it a home-grown status.

For our interest, how would the perception of Christianity as a foreign approach to spirituality advance or hinder our mission of making Cultural Chinese disciples of Christ? Has this negative reputation of the Christian faith changed today among Mainland Chinese? While the church in China has grown exponentially in the last few decades, I have found that the question still remains — can we find common grounds between the Christian faith and the Chinese culture? What about Diaspora Chinese globally? Is it truly the case that Jesus and his teachings are alien to the Cultural Chinese mind?

It is with all these questions and challenges in mind that the idea of this book came into being. While I am aware there exist many similar resources that deal with this theme, I am hoping that this book would present another angle to bridge the values of Cultural Chinese with the message of the gospel. However this is not an apologetics resource in the conventional sense. When one is engaging a Cultural Chinese, apologetics in the traditional sense may not get you very far as, often for them, truth and falsehood are subjective matters. Not that the question of truth is unimportant or irrelevant. Rather, a Cultural Chinese expresses a theory of truth that is appropriate to his culture.

Expert in world religions, Winfried Corduan, once quipped about the sense of truth among Cultural Chinese: "A correspondence theory of truth — namely that truth corresponds to your heart."[16] In other words, if you believe it in your heart, then it is truth. From a purely apologetics perspective, this can be most frustrating.

The Cultural Chinese's emphasis on maintaining peace in their relationships also further obscures the objectivity of truth. As the telling of truth may involve the unpleasantness of upsetting the other person, a genuine discussion of truth is hard to achieve. It is more virtuous to impress and remain pleasant than to discuss truthful matters and offend.[17] Hence there is a general reluctance to deal with the truth of matters directly and openly for fear of offending the other party.

What then is the most effective apologetics strategy that we should employ with a Cultural Chinese? Perhaps there is no need for one. After all, the Great Commission is not about finding an apologetic against all non-Christian worldviews but to witness about Jesus Christ to the world and make disciples in his name. Apologetics is just an approach where there is a need for us to clear away intellectual or cultural obstacles that may stand in the way of someone's understanding and acceptance of the gospel.[18]

The historical book of Acts records Paul's famous sermon in Athens. However, what preceded this event in Acts 17 was the accusation that Paul was preaching a foreign god to the Athenians:

> Now while Paul was waiting for them at Athens, his spirit was provoked within him as he saw that the city was full of idols. So he reasoned in the synagogue with the Jews and the devout persons, and in the marketplace every day with those who happened to be there. Some of the Epicurean and Stoic philosophers also conversed with him. And some said, "What does this babbler wish to say?" Others said, "He seems to be a preacher of foreign divinities" — because he was preaching Jesus and the resurrection. And they took him and brought him to the Areopagus, saying, "May we know what this new teaching is that you are presenting? For you bring some strange things to our ears. We wish to know therefore what these things mean."
> (Acts 17:16–20)

The Athenians called Paul a babbler who was presenting some weird ideas and they wanted to learn more about these ideas. Of course our audience may not be as interested in our message as the Athenians for, after all, the pragmatism of the Cultural Chinese would have no time for such endeavors! Instead, like Paul, we need to figure out if there is a way to locate some of their values within the Christian worldview.

If we are to relevantly share the Christian faith with the over 1.3 billion Cultural Chinese in the world, we need to understand their worldview. The onus is on us to learn and study about the Cultural Chinese worldview and their cultural expressions. We need to consider how to ask probing questions tactfully and learn to listen attentively as we seek the help of the Holy Spirit to discern the core issues at hand. We must learn how to articulate the gospel in terms that are attractive and significant to this quarter of the world's population.

This aptly describes the goal of this book. However there is no shortcut to our goal. In order for us to understand the Cultural Chinese worldview, we must take the winding path that leads us past the bamboo forest of ideas and philosophies that have so entrenched and formed the soul of the Cultural Chinese. Or, as in the words of my former boss, Dr. Ravi Zacharias, "In India there is a saying that you can touch your nose directly or you can touch your nose the long way around. And for some people, you need to go the long way around to reach them. It's a long road, but it's often the only road." Hence this book is the long way, but I believe it is also the road that is lined with fewer obstacles than you would encounter on many other shortcuts.

We will begin our journey on this winding path with the persuasion that we need to rethink our message and faith — that we need to start perceiving our faith as well as the gospel as a worldview or a metanarrative. Next we will go on a fast rollercoaster ride into the past to survey the key historical figures and events (Laozi, Kongzi and the advent of Buddhism) to decipher how they have contributed to the formation of the Cultural Chinese worldview. We will then take a closer look at Confucius's ideals — where we will begin to recognize how familiar they are to many of us. In the final chapter of this book, we will discuss the facets of Confucius's ideals that are parallel to what God had intended for his creation and how Confucius had fallen short of proposing the right path towards that end.

Blessed with the privilege of retrospection, we now know that there is only one way: "*Jesus said to him, 'I am the way, and the truth, and the life. No one comes to the Father except through me. If you had known me, you would have known my Father also. From now on you do know him and have seen him.'*" (John 14:6–7)

CHAPTER 2

Rethinking the Good News

Never forget what Jesus did for you. Never take lightly what it cost Him. And never assume that if it cost Him His very life, that it won't also cost you yours.

Rich Mullins

A story is told by my former colleague, L.T. Jeyachandran, of his experience with a group of pastors: when asked who are the ones who are more challenging to work with, the pastors unanimously agreed that Christians, the ones in their respective churches, are the ones who give them most problems — much more than non-believers. Perhaps you're not surprised by this response at all. Haven't we all had the experience where we're astonished by the discovery that one of our most difficult co-workers is a fellow Christian? I remember years ago my sister, before she became a believer, would complain to me about a particular client she worked for. I agreed that her client was indeed a mean person but imagine my shock when we discovered that this man is someone I knew and that we even went to the same church! In fact, he was a church elder!

In response to the pastors' reaction, Jeyachandran went on to suggest that often Christians are more difficult than we expect because of a curtailed understanding of what it means to be a follower of Christ. You see, when the altar call to salvation is made from the pulpit, the audience is asked if they were ready if they were to die the next day. Naturally this appealed to their fear and many would accept the salvation that Jesus offers so that they would go to heaven should they pass on the next day. But in all probability, none of them would die the next day and they would go on their merry old way of life. As a result, we end up with many "Christians" who know how to die as a Christian but do not know how to live as one.

A.W. Tozer once commented that it is possible that there is a wrong belief that exists in evangelical Christian circles that we can choose to accept Christ only because we need him as Savior and that we can postpone our obedience to him as Lord as long as we want to.[1] In the same vein, the late Dallas Willard is convinced that there is this belief in evangelical churches today that it is quite reasonable to be a "vampire Christian." A vampire Christian is one who says to Jesus: "I'd like a little of your blood, please. But I don't care to be your student or have your character. In fact, won't you just excuse me while I get on with my life, and I'll see you in heaven." But can we really imagine that this is what it means to be a follower of Jesus?

The Great Commission charged by the Lord Jesus in Matthew 28 is not new to us: "*Go therefore and make disciples of all nations, baptizing them in the name the Father and of the Son and of the Holy Spirit, teaching them to observe all that I have commanded you.*" Commonly preached to exhort us towards missions, most of us are aware of our task in evangelism and discipleship. However I have often wondered two things about this commission: one, in order for us to "make disciples" needn't we be disciples first ourselves? Second, part of the challenge of the Great Commission is to preach the Good News. But are we clear on what exactly our message is — why it is good and why it matters? Why should anyone give our message a hearing and even consider believing it to be true?

All too often when we share the gospel, we condense it into a simple transactional narrative that affirms the basics of our faith: "God loves us and has a wonderful plan for us. But we have sinned and are therefore separated from Him. Jesus Christ on the cross is the answer to our sinful state, and if we will accept him as our personal savior, we will have eternal life." This transactional narrative surely captures the essence of the gospel and affirms the basics of our faith but it does not give a wholistic presentation of what the gospel is about. In fact, such a simplified presentation can wrongly convey the idea that the gospel is primarily about our own fulfillment and satisfaction — "God loves YOU and has a wonderful plan for YOU." A truncated message like this seems to place us and not Jesus in the center of the gospel. With such a "gospel" we end up with Christians who want access to heaven from what Jesus has done for them on the cross but who may not necessarily be keen on the lordship of Christ.

On the contrary, the heart of both the Old and New Testaments is the fulfillment of God's plan. The story of our redemption is God's complete and multifaceted movement through history among all people and nations. This cannot be reduced to the mere background of "God's wonderful plan for *YOU*" without compromising the reach and heart of God's redemptive mission.

We must not neglect to see that the truth of the Christian faith is rooted in thousands of years of the history of humanity and that is what makes it so relevant to each of us individually and corporately. The person of Christ and the salvation that he offers is meaningful to us today only because Christ is historical. If we look at the other religions around us, for example Hinduism and Buddhism, history is cyclical as, after one dies, one is reincarnated or rebirthed. In addition, the historicity of Gautama has never been a central issue for Buddhism.[2]

Theologian Paul Tillich once had a fascinating and telling conversation with some Japanese Buddhists when he visited Kyoto in 1960. When asked: "If some historian should make it probable that a man of the name Gautama never lived, what would be the consequence for Buddhism?" The Buddhist scholars responded that since the *dharma kaya* (the body of truth) is eternal, the historicity of Gautama is irrelevant. Therefore, history is of no real significance or meaning. Events are just occurrences.

On the contrary, within the Christian faith, what Jesus teaches is significant only because of who he is and what he has done, his death and resurrection. The past and the future are very important for Christians because they give us hope and meaning for our present. The past grants us perspective by providing us meaning to our present existence. The future, on the other hand, gives us hope because no matter what hardship we are going through today, it will soon pass into a future when we will be in complete fellowship with God and when all tears will be wiped away.

As I write this, various social media are being virally updated with posts of Christians who are either brutally murdered or violently persecuted for the simple fact that they profess to be followers of Jesus. As we weep in sorrow and rage in rightful anger with the families of those who are martyred, we are comforted by the wondrous hope that John saw in his vision on Patmos:

> *Then I saw a new heaven and a new earth, for the first heaven and the first earth had passed away, and the sea was no more. And I saw the holy city, new Jerusalem, coming down out of heaven from God, prepared as a bride adorned for her husband. And I heard a loud voice from the throne saying, "Behold, the dwelling place of God is with man. He will dwell with them, and they will be his people, and God himself will be with them as their God. He will wipe away every tear from their eyes, and death shall be no more, neither shall there be mourning, nor crying, nor pain anymore, for the former things have passed away." (Revelation 21:1–4)*

Unfortunately, many of us have lost our perspective of the grand narrative of reality. Many today are suffering from a historical amnesia where we have lost our interest and understanding of history. This ahistorical climate we are living in is affecting the way we perceive truth in relation to reality. One reason why novels like the *Da Vinci Code* of a few years ago and news of the discovery of the various "gospels" (Gospel of Judas, Gospel of Mary, Gospel of Thomas, etc.) intrigue us and give us cause to be skeptical is that history, the past, has no existential meaning for a lot of us. It is especially troubling to know that this ahistorical mood permeates our churches today.

There is unfortunately a compounded illiteracy when it comes to church history and historical theology. This does not bode well for the adherents of the Christian faith because ultimately the message of Christianity is about the acts of God in time and space and, most significantly, the acts of God in Christ that took place in real time past. Therefore, as Christians, we must appreciate the history of Christianity. When we do so, we are remembering the historical character of our faith which in turn would testify to the all-encompassing sovereignty of God. As Lesslie Newbigin correctly maintains: "The Christian faith is — as often said — a historical faith not just in the sense that it depends on a historical record, but also in the sense that it is essentially an interpretation of universal history."[3]

Sadly, many Christians view their belief in God as merely a set of doctrines or a moral code. By doing so, they have created a false dichotomy between their spiritual beliefs and other facets of life. Or they have allowed their belief system to be reduced to little more than private feelings and experience, completely divorced from objective facts and even reality.[4]

Chuck Colson rightly comments, "The Christian faith cannot be reduced to John 3:16 or simple formulas. Christianity cannot be limited to only one component of our lives, a mere religious practice or observance, or even a salvation experience."[5] In other words, true Christian faith is more than a relationship with Jesus expressed in personal piety, church attendance, prayer meetings, Bible study and works of charity/missions. Rather, Christianity is a way of perceiving and comprehending all reality. It is a worldview. As such, we must begin to perceive our faith that way — as the all-encompassing truth, the root of everything else. It is ultimate reality.

Contrary to what many may believe, *worldview* is not an abstract philosophical category. While worldviews are defined and evaluated using intellectual categories and terms, they are inextricably linked to lived experience and behavior — they are practical and have to do with the lived reality. They are the sum total of our beliefs about the world that directs our daily decisions and actions.[6]

Of all the definitions of a worldview proffered by philosophers, my preferred one is by John H. Kok that aptly captures what a worldview is:

> A worldview may well be defined as one's comprehensive framework of basic beliefs about things, but our talk (confessed beliefs or cognitive claims) is one thing, and our walk (operative beliefs) is another and even more important thing. A lived worldview defines one's basic convictions; it defines what one is ready to live and die for.[7]

A worldview can also be likened to a pair of glasses through which we see the world. If you wear prescription glasses you will know how frustrating it is when you are wearing a pair that's not rightly prescribed. The right glasses would present the world as it really is, while others would have a distorting or blurry effect. This reminds me of a recent fashion fad where one wears a pair of glasses that has either no glass or glass that is non-prescription. In other words, it's purely for cosmetic purposes — the pair of glasses do nothing to help the wearer see better.

In using the analogy of a pair of glasses further, Udo Middelmann in his book *Christianity vs. Fatalistic Religions* adds, "What we need is not a set of glasses that merely paints a pretty picture or one that everyone agrees with. We need glasses that put reality into focus. We need to see more clearly and recognize the sharp edges of reality."[8] Hence it is important to examine if our glasses reveal, enhance or distort. The right worldview will help us understand and interpret the events and ideas that we experience accurately.

It is not merely a vision of life but a vision for life as well. How we view life affects the kind of life we live. A story told by Middelmann illustrates this clearly.[9]

In Muru, a small town east of Nairobi, lies a missions hospital. Next to the hospital were three large steel tanks. During the two rainy seasons, typical in East Africa, a low wall formed like the letter "Y" channeled water into a small aqueduct. This would fill the tanks with rainwater. Two seasons a year, more than 450,000 gallons of water would be stored this way. It was enough for the needs of the hospital, its patients and their families for the six dry months annually.

Life was very different in the village nearby where life was less stable. The principal of a school at the bottom of the mountain explained how the lives of his students were challenged in the areas of education, healthcare and supervision. Whenever the dry season came, a great migration would take place. When the rain stopped, the animals would graze according to the receding river. The families with their children would follow their animals. The classrooms would empty slowly from 450 pupils to fewer than 100. Education was controlled by nature's seasonal changes. It was difficult to attain stability when human life and survival were determined by nature.

When asked about the water tanks which had been installed decades earlier under European influence, the principal said that this was a great idea and an interesting way to deal with the deprivation of water, but he also saw it as very Western and not how the local people would have chosen to live.

What was happening here was not merely the difference in Western or African ways of doing things. The creative effort to store rain water was the expression of a different way of perceiving reality — of nature, people and life itself. Behind the initiative and innovation by means of simple tools and available resources was a view of the world that was distinct from the traditionalism or fatalism of most religions.[10]

The difference between the two outlooks on life in Muru did not lie in their knowledge or the lack of it. There was no difference in the availability of material resources either. The difference clearly displayed a profoundly different perspective of the value of life — different views of human beings in the midst of the hardships of the real world. One outlook facilitated ingenuity and innovation, while the other led to fatalism.[11] One accepted nature as the final authority while the other, God. Without the biblical understanding and perception of all areas of life, our efforts to bring about transformation will reap only limited results because, ultimately, it is necessary for the hearts and minds of people to be addressed, informed, nourished and corrected for lasting transformation.[12] Both material needs and moral/cultural impediments must be overcome for effective and lasting help.

Poverty results not only from the cruelty of many people to each other but also from a poverty of ideas about life, work and meaning. While material needs are more evident, poor ideologies that are the root of material poverty must also be addressed urgently. Hence, any mercy or relief work that is done in the name of Jesus must involve careful study of religious, intellectual, social, political and cultural ideas that war against the human being. Aid in relief and development, education and healthcare, and business and social involvement alone are inadequate to achieve radical and sustained transformation.[13]

If a worldview is the sum total of our beliefs about reality, then every worldview must at least be able to answer these basic questions: Where did we come from, and who are we (creation)? What has gone wrong with the world (fall)? What can we do to fix it (redemption)?[14] While these may not necessarily be the kind of questions we ponder with friends over *chai* or *dimsum* and *oolong* tea, they form the basis of our perception of the world and govern our behavior and decisions. G.K. Chesterton, the jolly late-nineteenth-century writer gives a fitting analogy (in *Heretics*):

> But there are some people, nevertheless — and I am one of them — who think that the most practical and important thing about a man is still his view of the universe. We think that for a landlady considering a lodger, it is important to know his income, but still more important is to know his philosophy. We think that for a general about to fight an enemy, it is important to know the enemy's number, but still more important to know the enemy's philosophy. We think the question is not whether the theory of the cosmos affects matters, but whether, in the long run anything else affects them.[15]

In addition, if our worldview is the sum of our beliefs then it must change when our beliefs are altered. Our worldview is therefore dynamic. When we experience a crisis or sudden insight or realization, our worldview could shift. Sometimes, this shift is so drastic, you may even call it a conversion. In fact, this is exactly what ought to happen at conversion. What would a conversion be if not for a total realization that what we previously believed about reality — God, meaning, purpose, etc. — is flawed or downright wrong? After all, what is a conversion if not a revolution of our worldview?

What is prevalent in the culture around us will also inevitably have an effect on our worldview. One of the things that culture does, according to Kevin Vanhoozer, is that it cultivates.[16] Culture cultivates the human spirit. In other words, culture is a powerful means of spiritual formation. Unfortunately many of us are unaware of culture's impact on the formation of our worldview. Yet, as Vanhoozer warns, disciples of Jesus cannot afford to sleepwalk their way through everyday life. Those who confuse the truth with pathetic imitations would make very poor ambassadors for the true Christ.[17]

Culture informs us and ultimately forms our beliefs in what is true, good and beautiful. I find this very self-evident in my own life:

For years growing up, I struggled with the appearance of my eyes — they are what the Chinese call single-eyelid eyes (women's magazines now call them "monolids"). I hated how my eyes look — they are small and it is impossible to properly put any eye make-up on — a real concern if you were female. "It's like clandestine eyeliner," my husband once quipped. If you are a Westerner reading this, you might be wondering what single-eyelid eyes are and why are they so abhorrent, but if you were an Oriental Asian, you would know exactly what I am referring to. Growing up, my idea of beauty included a set of wide, double-eyelid eyes. My idea of beauty was formed by what my culture projected as ideal, and further reinforced by my exposure to media that flaunted models of big, beautiful, double-eyelid eyes on their glossy pages as well as on the big screen.

Then entered my Caucasian date (who is now my husband) who thought that I'm absolutely beautiful. But I rebutted the compliment by highlighting that I have single-eyelid eyes. "What do you mean? How are your eyes different from mine?" he asked. It turned out that he had never noticed how my eyes were different from anyone else's. In fact, upon further discussion, he did not realize that there existed such a thing as single-eyelid eyes and why they are regarded as less than perfect! I then recalled a good friend's earlier remark that despite my discontent, Westerners will find my eyes exotic and attractive. How true. At least one did, and married me!

Humor aside, the story of my eyes illustrates culture's power in cultivating our perceptions and what we believe about reality. In fact, Vanhoozer adds that just as culture casts ideal forms for our bodies, so it forms ideals for our spirit.[18] This means, culture cultivates and forms the kind of person we are — our character, our actions and reactions (that are based on our beliefs), and our habits. That is why it is imperative that we pay attention to what we allow to shape our worldview. Popular culture? What kind of movies do you spend most time watching? Which websites do you frequently surf? Which artistes do you enjoy listening to? What sort of books are you reading?

As our choices are shaped by what we believe is real and true, right and wrong, good and beautiful, in every action that we take, we are doing one of two things: we are either helping to create a hell on earth or helping to bring down a foretaste of heaven. We are either contributing to the broken condition of the world or participating with God in redeeming and transforming the world to reflect his righteousness. In other words, we are either advancing the rule of Satan or establishing the reign of God.[19]

Spying Out the Land

When I first moved to Turkey to be involved in church planting, I was discouraged from engaging in any form of ministry until I had learned more about the Turkish culture and at least spoke some of the local language. While it was frustrating initially, it did not take me long to appreciate the wisdom of such a requirement. Just like cross-cultural missionaries throughout the history of modern mission, when they are sent to a foreign country or context, they would first spend time examining and learning the language and the culture so that they can share the gospel in a way that is meaningful and relevant to those they are trying to reach. It is not enough to just know the content of the gospel — it is important to understand the culture in which we are to be witnesses. We commonly (and sometimes thoughtlessly) assert that Jesus is the answer. But lest that becomes a cliché, do we know what is the question (or, perhaps, *questions*)?

Our task in evangelism is therefore two-fold: first, before we set out to make disciples, we are to do some housekeeping. We are to become conscious of our worldview. Our personal background and historical setting would have no doubt influenced our reading of Scripture and our view of the world. Our worldview shapes our theology that would in turn influence how we understand and contextualize the gospel.[20] Jackson Wu points out that differences in theology are often differences in emphasis. And the difference in emphases is most likely caused by our difference in culture. There are always traces of culture in one's theology. In short, we need to develop our biblical worldview, fully grasp what the gospel is about and understand our cultural context if we are to be followers of Jesus who take our discipleship seriously.[21]

This leads us to the second part of our two-fold task of evangelism — it is not enough for us to merely quote various Scripture verses or proof texts in our evangelism, or to compare our beliefs to the beliefs of other religions and assert that we are right. We have to set out and scope out their land — we must be able to understand where our non-Christian friends are coming from, their basic assumptions about the world, and think about how we can counter those false assumptions. (Of course we must also be able to give reasons for our own assumptions and beliefs and defend them!) We need to know what are the roadblocks to people coming to faith. To engage the unbelieving world effectively, we need to understand the ideas that compete for people's minds and hearts.

You would be mistaken to assume that you already know the ultimate concerns and beliefs of your neighbor. It might surprise you to know that you do not need to travel very far to engage in some form of cross-cultural conversation. Kevin Vanhoozer aptly describes this reality:

> My everyday world includes Dostoyevsky, Brahms, PBS, conversation around the dinner table, doctoral students, philosophical problems, and Christian doctrine as well as grocery shopping, getting gas, going to movies, and balancing the checkbook. My neighbor's everyday world, however, seems to me like a planet far, far away that orbits around American Idols, football players, and fast-food, as well as playing the lottery, surfing the Internet, and watching porn. One need not travel far to enter other worlds.[22]

Hence an essential first step to cross-cultural ministry is to understand our audience and the cultural world they inhabit — we examine the worldview; seeking to understand its values, customs and patterns of thinking. Then we look for the significance of various cultural texts while refraining from quick judgments or reductionism.[23]

This is exercised in the hope of finding common ground. If there are areas of agreement between a worldview/religion and the Christian faith then possibilities of bridge building can be explored. For example, the atheist and the Christian both believe that evil and suffering are real and must be eradicated. Similarly, a conversation with a Buddhist could see us agreeing with their diagnosis of the problem of suffering — our attachment to the things of the world (1 John 2:15) but the solution to the problem proposed by the two belief systems are radically different.

The common concerns that we have with the Atheist and the Buddhist could serve as a point of connection with them as we lead into a deeper discussion about the truth and falsity of the beliefs we have about reality.

When we finally present the gospel, it immediately becomes highly relevant and attractive (to a world longing for lasting hope) because it is communicated as a worldview narrative (relating to all of life) instead of a reductionist version of a non-contextual transaction that merely saves us from hell to heaven after death.

One of the earliest evangelism methods I learned in church was to present my testimony of how God had transformed me and given me true meaning and purpose for my life. I was taught that when I shared from a personal experience, it would be difficult for the non-believer to negate what God had done in my life. While this worked a few times, it did not take long for me to encounter a Buddhist who had a similar testimony of the good that meditation had brought into her life. I realized that merely sharing my personal story as the reason for my belief in Jesus was insufficient. Though the positive transformation that I experienced after becoming a Christian is real, my Buddhist neighbor could easily relate her parallel experience of how spiritual discipline according to Buddha's Eightfold Path had brought her inner peace and strength.

It soon became clear to me that any witnessing that is limited to merely sharing my personal testimony without the validation of the truthfulness of the gospel is inadequate. Harold Netland, who used to be a missionary in Japan, agrees that any use of personal stories in our evangelism should be supported by other validating factors since "Christian witness based merely upon personal experience or the pragmatic benefits of conversion would have little to say concerning why my neighbor ought to abandon Buddhism and embrace the Christian faith."[24]

In the Asian cultural setting, the testimony of our subjective experience with Jesus, apart from reference to the objective truthfulness of the Christian faith, is insufficient. The truth-value of the gospel is both personal and universal. It is universal in that it is objectively true for all people, regardless of where they are located.

Fundamentally, the Christian faith is grounded in the fact that the One who created the heavens and earth has revealed truth about himself and humanity. This truth that is centered in the person and work of Jesus Christ needs to be both believed and acted upon if we are to be restored to a proper relationship with God. The universality of the Christian gospel lies in the fact that every person, irrespective of ethnicity, culture or religion, is a sinner and in need of redemption by God's grace, and that God desires all to be saved through a particular person, Jesus Christ, the absolutely unique incarnation of God who took upon himself the sins of the world.[25] Therefore, the justification for such an exclusive view of God requires more than our personal experience with Jesus.

Throughout the apostle Paul's ministry, he is often recorded as reasoning, presenting evidence and trying to rationally persuade others to become Christians. Though precise in the way he shared the message of Christ's atonement, he never failed to emphasize the truth and universal relevance of the gospel and he did not merely appeal to felt needs. We can take a cue from his encounter with the Athenians in Acts 17:

> So Paul, standing in the midst of the Areopagus, said: "Men of Athens, I perceive that in every way you are very religious. For as I passed along and observed the objects of your worship, I found also an altar with this inscription, 'To the unknown god.' What therefore you worship as unknown, this I proclaim to you. The God who made the world and everything in it, being Lord of heaven and earth, does not live in temples made by man, nor is he served by human hands, as though he needed anything, since he himself gives to all mankind life and breath and everything. And he made from one man every nation of mankind to live on all the face of the earth, having determined allotted periods and the boundaries of their dwelling place, that they should seek God, and perhaps feel their way toward him and find him. Yet he is actually not far from each one of us, for 'In him we live and move and have our being'; as even some of your own poets have said, 'For we are indeed his offspring.'
>
> Being then God's offspring, we ought not to think that the divine being is like gold or silver or stone, an image formed by the art and imagination of man. The times of ignorance God overlooked, but now he commands all people everywhere to repent, because he has fixed a day on which he will judge the world in righteousness by a man whom

he has appointed; and of this he has given assurance to all by raising him from the dead." (Acts 17:22–31)

The text suggests that Paul found himself in Athens among a community that was highly pluralistic, with worldviews that were very diverse and distant from the Judeo-Christian tradition. It was not in Paul's plan to be in Athens at that time but he was escaping persecution in Macedonia and ended up having to wait for his other companions there. Interestingly, the cultural and religious environment in Athens at that time was not very different from the cultural and religious environment of Asia today. Idolatry was prevalent and there existed just as many different types of religions and philosophies. Two popular systems of belief in Athens at that time were the philosophies of Epicureanism and Stoicism.

Epicureans believed that the main goal in life was pleasure and the greatest pleasure was from living a life that was free from pain, superstitious fears and anxiety about death. The Epicurean's view of life sounds very familiar today, especially for us who live in urban centers in Asia. For example, it is becoming more common for young, middle-class couples in urban centers to no longer want to have children as they are seen as a liability. They do not want anything, including their children, to be in the way of them enjoying the material fruits of their labor. They want to be able to travel and indulge in a life of luxury goods which the advent of children would so often obstruct. Epicureans also believed that the gods that existed had no interest in the lives of the people.

Stoicism, on the other hand, held to a pantheistic concept of God — very much like what orthodox Hindus and Buddhists believe about God. Just like the concept of the Force in *Star Wars*, pantheists believe God is in all and is all, and all is God. God and the universe are one. There is ultimately only one reality, only one being that exists and we are all part of that being. In other words, we are all part of that divine reality/being.

As Paul observed the situation in Athens, he was compelled to present the claims of Christ to those around him — how could he not since God's will for humanity had been revealed to him. He starts by taking a point of contact in the altar that he saw. We can truly learn from Paul's way of presenting the gospel where he starts from a common ground with his hearers and then leads them to accept the work and person of Jesus as the goal of God's redemptive work for humanity. How does he do this?

First, Paul starts his presentation by claiming that it was God who created the heavens and the earth and everything in it. Not only did he create the first man, he subsequently made all nations through this man. However, after his act of creation, he did not leave his creation alone. Rather, he sustained them and gave all men life and breath. Yet, man chose to rebel against his creator. The rebellion of man led to the fall of man — original sin. Since then, sin has entered into the human race and most parents would know that we don't have to teach our children to lie, they somehow have the natural capacity to do so (Rom. 5:12, 14).

However, God foreknew the rebellion of man and in his love and mercy initiated his plan to redeem us from death as a result of sin. Throughout the Old Testament, which spans a few thousand years, we see God's hand upon nations and individuals as they fulfilled their role in God's progressive revelation of his plan for our redemption — Abraham (blessings of all nations through the chosen people of Israel), Moses (the Passover — a picture of the redeeming act of the sacrificial lamb), and others.

Then, in the New Testament, we see the fulfillment of the coming of the Messiah that was promised in the person of Christ. Jesus's mission, as prophesied hundreds of years before, was to shed his blood as a substitute for our guilt and shame — Isaiah 53 gives us a very vivid picture of what the Messiah had to go through for his people. John 19:30 records Jesus saying "*It is finished!*" as he dies on the cross. Indeed, what Jesus said was very appropriate as the climax of God's plan of redemption was finally reached. However, Jesus's death on the cross was not the end of the plan of God as his death alone would not bring about victory over sin and death if the resurrection had not taken place.

Writing to the church in Corinth (1 Cor. 15), Paul stressed the importance of the resurrection: without his resurrection, Jesus's death would have been just the death of a martyr or of an activist for a good cause, like Gandhi. Jesus's death is significant because he did not stay dead! After appearing to his many followers for 40 days, Jesus ascended into heaven. Jesus's ascension is pivotal for at least two reasons. One, in the same way he ascended into heaven he promises that he will return (Acts 1), and two, with the ascension comes the fulfillment of the promise of his presence with all who believe in him through the Holy Spirit. The coming of the Holy Spirit recorded in the book of Acts marked a new era of humanity — the age of grace.

G.K. Chesterton aptly captures the optimism of Jesus's resurrection in *The Everlasting Man*:

> *On the third day the friends of Christ coming at daybreak to the place found the grave empty and the stone rolled away. In varying ways they realized the new wonder; but even they hardly realized that the world had died in the night. What they were looking at was the first day of a new creation, with a new heaven and a new earth; and in a semblance of the gardener God walked again in the garden, in the cool not of the evening but the dawn.[26]*

Note the breadth of Paul's message in Acts 17: after he courteously esteemed the Athenians' reverence for God, he prefaced his message by going back to the beginning — to the drama of creation — and identified the Creator of all as one who is transcendent and personal, holding command over the history of his creation. Then he went on to describe God's mercy in relation to the human condition setting the stage for the climax of his message — redemption through the death and resurrection of Jesus, and the need for all people to repent.[27]

In his speech Paul did not explicitly quote the Hebrew scripture. Instead, he quoted from the writings of pagan Greek poets with whom his audience was familiar (Acts 17:28). Paul sets the example for us that sometimes we need not quote verses from the Bible outright to bring across the redemption message. There will be instances when the audience will be more receptive to the truth of the gospel when familiar contextual expressions like cultural folk stories or anecdotes are used as illustrations.[28]

In addition, even though Paul understood that God's judgment of man's sinfulness is crucial, he did not start his speech at Athens on that point. Rather, Paul presented the grand history of humanity to demonstrate the relevance of the Christian worldview and how the message of redemption is true to its own claim. This is a noteworthy point for us who engage Cultural Chinese. Most Cultural Chinese would find the idea of sin and our sinfulness plainly offensive. If that is the case, is there another way we can bring across the idea of our sinful condition that they would readily identify with? This is what we will spend the next few chapters exploring.

I started this chapter by suggesting that if we were to go and make disciples (as commissioned by Christ), we would need to first be disciples of Jesus ourselves. I am going to assert further that the kind of disciples we make for Christ will be determined by the kind of disciple we are. Vampire Christians beget vampire disciples. Sleepwalking Christians beget sleepwalking disciples.

Hence, if we heed the call of Paul (Rom. 12:2 *"Do not be conformed to this world, but be transformed by the renewal of your mind..."*) and the command of Christ (Matt. 24:19 *"Go and make disciples..."*) seriously, we must not only take our faith seriously but also begin to consider our faith within the framework of the big narrative of the story of humanity. Ultimately, the Christian way has to be preached and defended on the basis that it is the only true and right way to live and to interpret all of life. It is only when we do so, that we will see why it is so compelling that we will want to live out this truth. And not only that, but also to long to share this good news with those around us. It is only when we see the truthfulness and relevance of the gospel from a worldview perspective that we can proclaim along with Paul, *"Woe to me if I do not preach the gospel!"* (1 Cor. 9:16).

CHAPTER 3

Religion of the Way: Daoism

*But there are some people, nevertheless —
and I am one of them — who think that the
most practical and important thing about a
man is still his view of the universe.*

Gilbert Keith Chesterton

Untangling the Roots of the Cultural Chinese

While I have a personal disdain for much of contemporary corporate or business jargon, I believe there is one that is fitting to what we are trying to achieve in this chapter: peeling the onion. Peeling the onion refers to learning more about something or someone by peeling back the layers. This is where we scope out the landscape of the Cultural Chinese soul to understand their basic assumptions about the world, and think about how we can counter those false assumptions.

For us to truly understand the Cultural Chinese, we must start from Laozi, Confucius and Buddha because our present is intimately woven with the past. Hence, to engage the unbelieving Cultural Chinese effectively, we need to understand the ideas that have nurtured their historical, cultural, and social realities, as well as those that compete for their minds and hearts presently. We also need to learn about the roadblocks that are standing in the way of them embracing the Christian faith as their own.

Many Cultural Chinese all over the world, regardless whether one is raised in Beijing, Singapore, Medan, San Francisco or Hong Kong, practice a plethora of rituals and are committed to obligations that seem to stem from similar values and beliefs about the world. While the philosophical and religious principles behind this common approach to life are not explicit, it is possible to detect the influences of the "Three Religions of the Orient" (*San Jiao*) on the worldview of the Cultural Chinese. The "Three Religions" (*San Jiao*) of the Chinese refer to the Religion of the Learned (Confucianism), Religion of the Way (Daoism), and Religion of Buddha (Buddhism). An appreciation of the philosophy of these three religions is essential to an understanding of the Cultural Chinese as they not only define the salient features of the Chinese civilization but have contributed greatly to the intellectual and moral aspect of the Cultural Chinese soul.[1]

Ancient Chinese Beliefs

Like most ancient civilizations, ancestral veneration, animism, as well as belief in spirits existed in ancient China, too. Also referred to as Shenism, we may not necessarily consider it as one of the main religious systems of the Cultural Chinese, but the Three Religions certainly emerged and grew in the soil of these traditional beliefs about reality. This is significant because these beliefs, in conjunction with the Three Religions, provide the basis for many of the Cultural Chinese traditions that are practiced till today — like *Qingming* (Chinese All Souls Day) and the Hungry Ghost Festival.

One of the key aspects of Shenism is the belief in a reality where spiritual beings intervene in every area of nature and the human world. Good spirits (*shen*) can hear and grant answers to human petitions, bring blessings and act to protect humans. Bad or evil spirits (*gui*), on the other hand, can cause diseases and bring trouble to humans. Hence, there exist many rituals that serve to either appreciate the good spirits or placate the evil ones. An early Chinese dictionary explains that *shen* are spirits of heaven associated with stars, mountains, and streams, and they exercise a direct influence on things in this world (*shen* is yang; while *gui* is yin). They are spirits intimately involved in the affairs of the world but their influence rarely stretches beyond that.[2] In other words, they are impotent when it comes to the fate of humans beyond life on earth.

Most scholars have observed that the majority of traditional religions venerate two kinds of spirits — ancestral and nature spirits.[3] Likewise, ancestral veneration is the other key aspect of traditional Chinese beliefs. If nature spirits were appeased, then how much more should the spirits of loved ones be venerated to ensure the guardianship and blessings of these ancestors? It is believed that these ancestral spirits do not simply reside in the realm of the dead but that they continue to maintain an integral relationship with their living descendants. As members of a family across the barrier of life and death, they continue to play an essential role in that community and their kinship status retains its importance and authority.[4] Subsequently, this veneration and respect for ancestors will feature strongly in Confucius's teaching regarding the Mandate of Heaven.

In addition to Shenism, another notion that predates the Three Religions is the belief in an omnipotent personal god who rules the world. There are good historical reasons to believe this god called *Shangdi* had already existed before the Shang era (1766–1027 BC).[5] Evident in ancient Chinese classics and literary works (poems), the term *Shangdi* was used to refer to the Supreme Lord who can receive worship of sacrifices, who can bless and the one whom the people should serve.

The Lord of Heaven is also the judge of all men and the source of happiness and goodness.[6] In all instances, the presiding king or emperor has a unique relationship with *Shangdi*, where the king is perceived to be the divinely anointed ruler and hence holds the key to the worship of *Shangdi*.

The emergence of a belief in *Shangdi* as the supreme god may be the result of theological meditations of shamans and other religious specialists who were in the royal entourage. Most scholars agree that *Shangdi* is not merely a deified ancestor of the king but the nonhuman high god who sanctions the dynasty.[7] In fact, Winfried Corduan goes further to conclude that *Shangdi* is indeed the god of original monotheism as opposed to an evolution of polytheistic beliefs in ancient China.[8] Whatever the origins of *Shangdi*, he remains an awesome, transcendent and supremely powerful being.

During the Zhou era (1122–256 BC) the term *Tian* began to replace the use of *Shangdi*.[9] It was used interchangeably with *Shangdi*. Though the literal meaning of the character is sky or heaven, it is not known to refer to a literal sky/heaven when used in a religious or spiritual context. It is similar to our use of "Thank heavens/Good heavens... ," which almost never implies that we are thanking the literal heaven. Throughout the *Shu* and the *Shi*, the ancient books of History and Poetry, the names *Tian* and *Shangdi* are constantly interchanged, in the course of the same chapter or paragraph, often in the same sentence.

Later, under the influence of Daoism and Buddhism, this classical notion of a personal divine being (*Tian*) began to shift to a more impersonal, monistic understanding of a Principle of Heaven (*Tian Li*). Come the era of Neo-Confucianism, the idea evolved further to a form of inner transcendence that can be achieved in the union of Heaven and man.[10] It will be evident that as we trace the transformation of the pursuit of external transcendence (in the form of worship of a Supreme deity) to inner transcendence, we see a correlation in the spiritual and philosophical movement of the times. Bearing this in mind, we now turn to the Three Religions of the Orient.

Daoism — The Religion of The Way

The oldest among the Three Religions is Daoism. While scholars have written scores of books on Daoism, none will deny the problem of trying to describe Daoism definitively. Many have attempted to provide a single normative definition of Daoism but their efforts fail as both the terms Dao as well as Daoism, as a system of thought and belief, are complex and widely divergent. However, Daoism's influence on the mystical and idealistic aspects of Cultural Chinese thinking and life cannot be disputed.

It has been traditionally accepted that Laozi was the founder of Daoism but not much has been really documented regarding this person, whether in history or in myth. This has led some scholars to doubt if Laozi actually existed.[11] Nonetheless it is traditionally accepted that he was born circa 604 BC, making him an older contemporary of Confucius. He is also traditionally credited as being the author of the whole book of *Laozi*, one of the principal texts of Daoism.[12] *Laozi*, the book, is popularly known today as the *Dao-de-jing*, which literally means the book of the way and its power.[13] The *Dao-de-jing* is probably one of the most frequently translated and yet most difficult of Chinese literature to decipher.[14] The composite nature of the book has led many to conclude that it was written by more than one person and was written no earlier than the fourth century BC.[15] This, of course, brings doubt to whether Laozi was really the writer of the *Dao-de-jing*.

So what is the Dao? The *Dao-de-jing* begins with these famous lines on what the Dao is:

> *The Tao that can be understood cannot be the primal, or cosmic, Tao, just as an idea that can be expressed in words cannot be the infinite idea. And yet this ineffable Tao was the source of all spirit and matter, and being expressed was the mother of all created things.*
>
> *Therefore not to desire the things of sense is to know the freedom of spirituality; and to desire is to learn the limitation of matter. These two things spirit and matter, so different in nature, have the same origin. This unity of origin is the mystery of mysteries, but it is the gateway to spirituality.*

As enigmatic as it may sound, the "definition" of the Dao simply indicates that it is indefinable and beyond words. It cannot be expressed. However, only as it is being expressed does it become a creative power. Nonetheless, the "definition" provided does indeed say something about the inexpressible Dao — that it is inexpressible![16]

While the *Dao-de-jing* is a small book of only 5,000 characters, it is notoriously difficult to translate as well as understand due to its obscure nature.[17] "... if one compares the various renderings, it is sometimes almost impossible to believe that the different translations are based upon the same text. It is sometimes an exasperating book... ," quipped Sinologist, H.G. Creel.[18]

The problems are similar with Daoism's second notable work, the *Zhuangzi*.[19] While it is traditionally believed that the man, Zhuangzi, is the author of the book (after all, the text bears his name!), the verdict is still out on its real authorship. Like the *Dao-de-jing*, the *Zhuangzi* was probably written by a group of individuals rather than by one individual.[20]

It is often challenging to work with ancient Chinese documents like the *Dao-de-jing* and *Zhuangzi* because they are difficult to place historically, hence compromising the contextual interpretation of the text. The ancient style and format of the writings further add to the obscurity of the text's meaning. Ironically, even Zhuangzi himself acknowledges the ambiguity of ancient writings in the text *Zhuangzi*: "Ordinarily, people can't avail themselves of the reserves of the mind of the Dao because everything, even the idea of the mind of Dao, is habitually filtered through the perceptions of the human mentality."[21]

The task of plainly defining the principle of Dao is also impossible because it is used in almost every school of Chinese philosophical thought and religion to refer to their various articulations accordingly.[22] In fact, even within the practice of Daoism itself, it is understood on two different levels: philosophical/metaphysical and religious/cultic.[23] If you were to pick up a book on Daoism from the bookstore or library, it is most likely that it is the contemplative and mystical philosophical Daoism that it discusses. Religious or popular Daoism, on the other hand, tends towards the cultic and magical; we will see why this is so at length.

Philosophical Daoism

In its philosophical form, Dao is used to metaphysically refer to the first principle and fundamental source of all existence. It is ultimate reality, the totality of all things. The Dao is the basic stuff out of which all things were made. It was simple, formless, desireless, without striving and supremely content. It existed before Heaven and Earth.[24] The first chapter of the *Dao-de-jing* describes Dao as "the original, the uncarved block, the unity behind all multiplicity."

Since all that exist — humanity and nature — proceed from Dao, then life and death, good and evil, are all parts of the harmonious order of the universe which is good.

This principle of harmony and good of the universe is depicted by the interaction of yin and yang — the negative and positive principles of nature and all of reality. As complementary opposites, the presence and interaction of yin and yang are central to all existence — they are divisible but inseparable and interdependent. As both yin and yang are manifestations of the universal Dao, they are morally neutral and complementary forces that appear together in various degrees in all things — man, nature and the physical world. Literally, yin means the shady north side of a hill and is characterized by an almost infinite list: cold, wet (rains and floods), dark, feminine, totally absorbent and etc. Yang, on the other hand, is the sunny south side of a hill and is characterized as light, bright, powerful, masculine, heat and etc.

For example, the interaction of yin and yang in nature is evident in the occurrence of night and day, dark and light, earth and heaven, cold and heat.[25] As yin and yang are complementary, the ideal is a dynamic balance between these two forces. All in nature is well when the yin and yang of nature are in harmony. Natural disasters, it is believed, occur when either yin or yang overwhelms and disrupts the harmony. Similarly, when the yin and yang harmony of our physical bodies is disrupted, we fall sick because the disharmony has weakened us.

Our Existential Problem
Daoists also believe the pain, suffering and discontent that we experience are due to our departure from the universal Dao. One could almost call this the Daoist version of the fall. Beginning from the emergence of humanity and everything else with it, we are drifting further and further away from the primal state of Dao and this has resulted in our discontentment.[26] The remedy to this fragmentation is for humanity and nature to merge into the Dao once again.[27] We can return to the "state of the uncarved block" by allowing ourselves to become one with nature without trying to change or alter our situation. This is the idea of *wu wei* (actionless action).[28]

When we become one with nature, our existential purpose can be sought and found by contemplating the world of nature and in communion with nature. The principles and laws of nature will illuminate us on how we ought to live in order to be absorbed back into the Dao. It is therefore not surprising that many who figure chiefly in early Daoism are farmers, fishermen and recluses.[29] The Daoist's desire to contemplate the works of the universe and ultimately identify himself with the vast cosmic process has led philosophers to describe it as a form of nature mysticism.[30] The pantheistic nature of Daoism is also quite unmistakable as it sees humanity, nature and all that exist as part of the metaphysical Dao.

Keep Calm and Be a Daoist

In the *Dao-de-jing*, the Dao is characterized as primitive, quiet (almost passive) but strong. Hence, for all who follow the Dao and seek to return to the Dao, they must embrace its quietness, simplicity and power by becoming "quietists".[30] In other words, when humanity abandons all attempts to strive for a better life for themselves or for society and retreat into *wu wei*, the Dao will manifest itself, and natural harmony for people as well as society will emerge by itself.[31]

The Daoist ideal is simplicity with the hope of ultimately returning to the Dao.[32] In fact, it is very clear that this call to simplicity means a Daoist should not strive for worldly power, position or honors but rather to live the life of a recluse.[33] All of life should not be forced or imposed but rather to wait and go with the rhythm and flow of the universe as it takes its course. However, it was rare to find dedicated mystics who would give up their life merely to contemplate the universe — even among early Daoists. Recognizing the restlessness of human nature, Creel critiqued the pursuit of contemplative Daoism:

> Now it is all very well to talk of caring nothing for the world's opinion, of not striving, being perfectly quiescent, remaining content with the lowest position in the world, and so forth. But human beings get tired of that sort of thing. And most of the Daoists were human, no matter how much they tried not to be.[34]

Creel seems to have brought up an important aspect of a worldview. Any worldview that is true ought to be livable in practical terms. In addition to rational criteria like consistency and coherence, factual adequacy, support by evidence, and so forth, Creel's observation suggests an important practical criterion in weighing competing worldviews that claim to be true. While the relationship between a worldview's truth and its livability may not be entirely clear, this practical criterion is based on a basic trust that human beings can discover the truths necessary for life, and that such truths are livable; the only other rational choice is despair.

Furthermore, the practical wisdom of such a criterion is in its recognition that only truths that we can act on and live by are ultimately of any help to us; it is only livable truths whose implications can be realized in our lives. This leads us to suspect that truth claims which do not meet this criterion, in the final analysis, probably are not true. After all, it seems more plausible to believe that belief systems that can only be described in words but cannot be lived in reality, do not actually correspond to reality, and thus are not true.

A related notion is that true belief systems will more likely enable human flourishing and the betterment of the human condition. Having a true understanding about the force of electricity enables us to harness it to light our homes, while having a true understanding of the body's nervous system enables us to use anesthesia to manage people's pain. The success of electricians and anesthesiologists alike in their work does not prove, but does give strong reasons for believing that the theory underlying their practice is true. A correct grasp of the truth about reality should enable us to cooperate with reality and improve our situation. There does not seem to be any reason why this should not also be the case for fundamental worldview issues than for practical ones. True worldviews should help us to live flourishing human lives as they are meant to be.

In addition, since Daoism advocates passivity (*wu wei*) in approaching life instead of being governed by social expectations and education, we will see how this stand against the imposition of social conventions is a direct contradiction to Confucius's ideal of human flourishing through the practice of virtues to strive towards becoming the Noble Man.

Over time, the practice of contemplative Daoism took on many organized forms and incorporated many observances that are believed to bring a person into union with the Dao. From its early contemplative form, Daoism evolved into a movement of cultic groups, sects and communities where each emphasized a different aspect or goal of the multifarious philosophy. This led to Daoism's syncretism with grassroot animistic beliefs.

Religious Daoism

The contemplative nature of philosophical Daoism also meant it was an open-ended system lacking in precise definition of its practice and beliefs. This inclusiveness appealed to individuals as well as groups who were interested in achieving a variety of goals. Over time, a multitude of sects, branches and communities emerged as part of the Daoist movement pursuing a wide variety of goals — from longevity, good health to social and political reform to spiritual insight. Through the centuries, the popularity of the many sects of religious Daoism waxed and waned. Today, the two more influential sects of Daoism are the Way of the Heavenly Masters (*Tianshi*) and the Way of Complete Perfection (*Quanshen*). The former is dominant in Taiwan while the latter is known for its monasteries — like the notable White Cloud Monastery in Beijing.[35]

The inclusive nature of this movement also resulted in a form of religious Daoism that disproportionately emphasized its mystical aspects — combining popular animistic mysticism and cultic search for immortality with the Daoist goal of union with the Dao. It is no wonder then that immortality and the pursuit of longevity are prominent themes in the history of Daoism and especially the more popular religious form of Daoism.[36]

As this form of Daoism had sprouted from the soil of ancestral worship and animistic beliefs, a pantheon of deities and immortals also soon emerged. Demigods and sages from legends and myths, and ancestral spirits are venerated and appeased because it is believed they hold the power to determine the fate of mortal humans. Some of these gods were human beings who were believed to have entered the world of gods as a result of their merit or ability to discover the elixir of immortality. The famous Eight Immortals is one such band which is deemed as exemplars of humanity.[37] In fact, these eight characters are often depicted in contemporary popular culture like films and comic books. They were even featured in a series of the *X-Men* comic book defending ancient China from the Chinese mutant Xorn.

In Cultural Chinese homes, these Daoist gods centered on the land.[38] Household gods that are commonly worshiped are the god of the kitchen as well as god of the earth, the sky and so on. These gods portrayed typically either in paintings or statuettes are fearsome in appearance and often depicted brandishing a huge sword ready for battle. I remember growing up in a household where there were three altars — one in the front yard for the god of the earth, one in the kitchen and a main altar for at least three gods in the living hall of the house; and I would diligently help to light joss sticks three times a day to appease them. On the first and fifteenth of the month, fruits and sometimes a whole poached chicken would be offered as an act of gratitude for their blessings and protection.

Today it is difficult to precisely point out Daoism's influence on the Cultural Chinese worldview since many of its practices have integrated with Confucianism and Buddhism. However, two areas that Daoism features dominantly are in the arts (including architecture) and Chinese medicine. For example, most growing up in a Cultural Chinese family would be warned that eating too much deep fried foods would heat your system and may result in you developing a sore throat. Hence, to maintain the yin and yang equilibrium, you will have to ingest something that would dampen the heating effect — like herbal tea or foods that have a cooling potency.

Similarly, acupuncture is practiced along the Daoist understanding of how the human body works. The equilibrium of the human body is imbalanced and ails when the flow of *qi* is blocked. When various points of the ailing body are pricked by the acupuncture needles, the flow of *qi* is released bringing relief and rectifying the body's yin and yang harmony. Today, traditional Chinese medical (TCM) practices are gaining acceptance and acclaim globally but many are unaware that Daoism is the principal influence of TCM physiology.

CHAPTER 4

Religion of the Learned: Confucianism

There were four things which the Master taught — letters, ethics, devotion of soul, and truthfulness.

Analects 7:24

Even though Confucianism is not the formal ideology of many Cultural Chinese today, its influence on their worldview, culture and social life remains powerful and undeniable due to its historical significance. For example, the weighty value placed on education and filial piety can all be traced to Confucius's teachings about how life ought to be ordered. While it is possible to detect the metaphysical footprints of Daoism and the existential projections of Buddhism in the Cultural Chinese worldview, the philosophy that has most profoundly shaped the Cultural Chinese's conception of life and reality has been this Religion of the Learned.

Confucianism is based on the philosophy and teachings of the ancient statesman, philosopher and educator Kongzi (551–479 BC). Just like most ancient personalities, it is difficult to separate the legend and tradition from historical facts about Confucius's life. When we disregard all the embellishment, we can be certain of a few things about Confucius: he was born in 551 BC in the small state of Lu which is in modern-day Shantung.

Not much is known about his ancestry but, as he testifies in his writing, as a young man he was, "without rank and in humble circumstances."[1] Before entering the civil service, he was a teacher. However, as he wanted to play an influential part in government, he took up a minor post in the government and worked his way up to become a minister before he was ousted as a result of court politics almost 30 years later. He loved to study and taught himself history and poetry.

Confucius grew up at a time of social chaos because the feudal system of the state was failing and disintegrating. As a result, families and individuals suffered while corrupt officials continued in their war for power and wealth. His personal experience and circumstances moved him to recognize that there was something very wrong with the world around him and that things needed to drastically change to get better.[2] He concluded that the only way for a society to experience peace and to flourish was by being a society that consisted of Noble Men who lived harmoniously with each other. It would be a society where everyone knew their place and lived accordingly.

Initially, Confucius's ideas were rejected as they were often critical of the aristocrats and ministers in power. His ideas on how the state as well as society ought to be run appeared to threaten the position of those in power. However, all this changed when Ji Kangzi, the head of the most powerful family in the state of Lu was impressed by Confucius's courage. Nonetheless, Confucius's tenure in state affairs was short-lived and in disappointment he lived out his life as an itinerant teacher.[3]

However, 200 years after Confucius's death, most, if not all, feudal rulers had subscribed to the philosophy in one way or another, especially during most of the Han period (circa 200 BC – AD 200) when Confucianism was the official ideology providing the state and society with a standard code of morals and prescribing precisely the nature of the relationship between those who govern and those who are being governed. Around AD 600, the civil service examination that tested aspiring government officials was established based on Confucian teachings. This form of Imperial examination lasted till 1905 when it was finally abolished. Hence it is no wonder that Confucianism's greatest contribution has been to the intellectual and ethical aspects of Cultural Chinese thinking and life.[4]

Many modern-day scholars describe Confucius's philosophy as humanistic. However, there are many reasons to believe otherwise. While it may not be explicit from his writings, we can easily conclude from his own account of spiritual evolution that Confucius was a religious man. He was likely a believer in Heaven as a personal God and was one who sought to understand and follow Heaven's will. As we examine the historical context in which he emerged, we see that he lived at a time when the ancient religious beliefs, with their emphases on divination and sacrifice, were questioned. Hence, it was perhaps the reaction of philosophers like Confucius who decided to distance themselves from such superstitious beliefs that heralded in a new age of ethical wisdom, thus contributing to the rationalist atmosphere of philosophical reflection.[5]

Though commonly described as one of China's Three Religions, Confucianism is ultimately not a religion into which you can "convert". Confucius was never regarded as a god and there were no Confucian priests or monks. Rarely were temples like the ones of Daoism and Buddhism constructed for Confucius. Instead, there were Confucian halls that were similar to ancestral halls, and in them tablets were displayed in place of the usual statuettes or images.[6] Rather than a religion, Confucianism is perceived as a way of life that consists of rituals that maintain the harmony of communities and societies.

Confucianism is essentially a Chinese tradition reflecting the Chinese attitude towards life and the world. Yao Xinzhong, a scholar in Confucianism, believes that Confucianism as typically understood is really more of a tradition that is generally rooted in Chinese culture and nurtured by Confucius and Confucians rather than a religion that was developed or founded. He believes that Confucius merely explored deeply and elaborated extensively on the basic principles of what was to become Confucianism.[7] Confucianism has subsequently spread to other parts of East Asia and flourished, but the Korean and Japanese forms of Confucianism are distinctively contextualized.

Confucianism is also often portrayed as utilitarian and this-worldly because its pragmatic principles focused on addressing the social dimension of human existence. In this way, Confucius's teachings were a profound shift from the traditional preoccupation with spirits to ideas on how we can transform ourselves — individually, as a society and ultimately as a state or nation — into something that would function properly.[8] In order for us to achieve that, Confucius taught that life ought to be ordered according to the following ideals and values.[9]

Self-cultivation — How to be Truly Human
Teaching on the centrality of the self, Confucius was especially concerned that man should develop as humans in the most moral sense.[10] Hence, the dominant idea of Confucianism is that every normal person can aspire to be the Noble or Superior Man. This Confucius ideal of a person is one whose life is guided by propriety (*li*), proper in personal and public conduct, respectful towards parents and superiors, just and humane (*ren*) to others.[11]

The ultimate goal of the Noble Man is to be superior to his fellows, if possible, but surely superior to his own past and present self. Confucius believed that this aspiration is realized through a moral code based on benevolence towards others, as well as proper education and practice of virtues. Therefore as a teacher, he did not discriminate according to social class — he made his teachings available to all. Opening the doors of education to people of all classes has since had a profound impact on Cultural Chinese culture, history and worldview.[12]

Mencius (372–298 BC) and Xunzi (313–238 BC) are probably two of Confucius's more famous followers. In reality, Confucius's followers, rather than the philosopher himself, wrote many of the ancient

Confucian texts. While both Mencius and Xunzi elaborated on and expanded the central ideas of Confucius, they seemed to disagree on the nature of humanity: Mencius believed that human nature is inherently good while Xunzi thought that we tend to be evil by nature.[13] Though they held very contradicting views about humanity, both agreed with Confucius that man can strive towards perfection through proper education and the practice of virtuous conduct.[14] This is the idea of self-cultivation.

Mencius thought that self-cultivation would help us realize the goodness within us so that we can truly live according to our nature. In contrast, Xunzi believed that despite our evil nature, we have the potential to become the Noble Man if we restrain our evil nature through ceremonials and rules of right conduct. This is achieved when our practice of virtues becomes habitual and our nature is transformed. In other words, the Noble Man is really what it means to be human.

A significant portion of the various Confucian texts, like the Analects, evolved around the characteristics of the Noble Man. He is one who exemplifies the highest of virtues like integrity, love for truth, and filial piety. He is a man of learning and of proper conduct:

> *A gentleman avoids seeking to satisfy his appetite to the full when he eats and avoids seeking comfort when he is at home. He is diligent in deed and cautious in word, and he associates with possessors of the Way and is put right by them. He may simply be said to be fond of learning.* (Analects 1:14)

It is no wonder then that education is so greatly valued and emphasized in societies that have been influenced by Confucianism like Singapore, Korea, Japan and, of course, China. For example, the Tiger Mom phenomenon. When Amy Chua published her book, *Battle Hymn of the Tiger Mother*, many in the enlightened postmodern West were shocked by her supposed harsh discipline on her children. However, many mothers I know in Singapore, Hong Kong and the like, simply shrugged at the idea that is neither new nor startling because tiger-parenting was simply the conventional way to parent our children. While I am not necessarily condoning extreme measures in disciplining our children, I am also aware that one of the contributing factors to the Tiger Mom phenomenon is our Confucian emphasis on education.

In my own childhood experience, my mother would endlessly remind me that a good education is the only way to a better life, and that I should take my studies seriously. My options were either study really hard, get exceptional grades and be admitted into an affordable state university in Malaysia, or end up working in a hair salon as a shampoo girl. An obvious choice, as you can imagine! The recent idea of a gap year where college-age children take a year off to figure out what they would like to do with their life would be unheard of and frowned upon. Besides, my responsibility as a child is to properly find a good job upon graduation and provide for my parents who have sacrificially brought me up.

A key virtue that Confucius emphasized is *ren*. Various terms have been used to describe it — humaneness and kindness towards others. Essentially it is the obligation or attitude to seek the welfare of others.[15] As we live out our prescribed roles in family and society, *ren* provides us the inner basis for doing so without slipping into legalism. *Ren* has sometimes been referred to as the Confucian Golden Rule:[16] "Do not do unto others what you would not have them do unto you." Confucius believed that if everyone practiced *ren* in their private and public lives, we would be able to attain the social harmony that would place us on a good stead towards the ideal society and state.

On the political level, he taught that the ruler or governing officials must rule with *ren* if he wants his subjects to obey him and behave humanely. As the ruler, he has been bestowed the Mandate of Heaven (*Tian Ming*) — the right to rule by heaven. The Mandate of Heaven is based on the conviction that Heaven has sovereign knowledge and power. As such, when the king is enthroned, it is believed that Heaven has placed him there and he is to rule in ways that are proper to his role — he must be kind and strive to meet the needs of his subjects as well as protect them.

However, should the ruler lose his *ren*, he will also lose the Mandate of Heaven and risk being usurped by his replacement. Interestingly, despite the cultural purge that was specifically targeted at Confucianism in the 1930s, in Communist China today there is a robust discussion for a political model that is based on humaneness in view of how purely democratic or purely authoritarian systems have failed in various parts of the world.[17]

Another fundamental Confucian virtue is *li* which is translated to mean propriety, etiquette, customs, rituals or simply the appropriate ways to behave or to do the right thing. *Li* is essentially the guiding principle on how we ought to conduct our daily life — from manners to behavior in all social situations. There is a proper way for everyone in their specific roles in society to carry themselves in every situation. These obligations have definitely influenced the way Cultural Chinese navigate the *guanxi* (relationship) in their social life. A simple definition of the concept of *guanxi* is "social relationships that are mutually beneficial and obligatory". Hence, within the Cultural Chinese context, it is always prudent to build and preserve *guanxi*.

While *guanxi* remains an intriguing part of the culture to outsiders, many Cultural Chinese negotiate the body language, proper greetings and social protocol naturally and seamlessly. I have only come to realize this innate ability of mine when I had to explain to my Caucasian husband the nuances of all that was going on at a cousin's wedding — especially all the tense undercurrents between various feuding family members!

Li concerns the practice of the norms of everyday life as well as rituals. However, rituals here are defined as the routines of daily life and not regimented religious practices. Perhaps the modern understanding of rituals would be disciplines. Confucius believed that the practice of rituals can ultimately form the virtues on which these rituals are built upon within individuals as well as in society. For example, nightly communal dinners with the family are a ritual in this sense and ought to be practiced as they strengthen familial relationships and eventually maintain the harmony in the family.

Hierarchy of Relationships

Confucius believed that the cultivation of the Noble Man would only be possible with a proper social environment that is conducive to inner harmony and the development of harmonious relationships with others. All efforts to be fully human would require the contributions of others into our lives as well as our fulfilling our roles and obligations to them. That is why Confucius viewed the self as the center of a network of relationships: family, friends, society, and state; and that the harmony of these five cardinal relationships must be maintained at all costs — ruler to ruled, father to son, husband to wife, brother to brother, and friend to friend.

1. *Father-son*: The foundation of society is the family and sometimes the family has been cited as the Cultural Chinese's religion. Some may argue that this is a dated observation of the Cultural Chinese but, with every Lunar New Year celebration, heart-tugging commercials premised on familial love and relationships flood television stations where the Lunar New Year is celebrated. While the values of filial piety and familial harmony may be losing their grip on the younger generation, there still exists a romantic sentiment about them and hence a real longing to return to these values that are deemed important and significant.

At the core of the family is the relationship between father and son. Based on the virtue of *ren*, fathers are to treat their sons kindly while sons are expected to relate to their fathers in respect. Confucius taught that filial piety is among the greatest of virtues and, as such, has to be shown towards both the living and the dead. The reasoning behind filial piety is simply that parents are honored because they are the origins of one's life.

The term "filial," meaning "of a son," denotes the respect and obedience that a son should show to his parents and, especially, to his father. This directive encompasses all parent-children relationships. This reverence also includes not causing his parents to lose face. Filial piety is an unconditional obligation and is to be shown regardless of whether the parents deserve it or not. Also, children are to meet the expectations of the parents even when the expectation is wrong. Specific duties are prescribed on how a child should relate to a parent and such duties are also extended to the dead. This teaching reinforces the practice of ancestral veneration, to which the living stood as sons to their forefathers.

The idea of the Mandate of Heaven (*Tian Ming*) also extends to familial relationships where the will and wisdom of elders in the family are deemed equivalent to the *Tian Ming*. As such, the living are to seek the will and guidance of their elders even after they have passed on from this world. While living, parents, in their wisdom and duty, are expected to help their children by making certain life decisions for them, e.g. career and marriage partner. Today, it would be unheard of for parents to make such decisions for their children. Young people would prefer to marry for love. However, in view of the rampancy of divorce, one wonders if there is not any wisdom in arranged marriages!

2. *Elder brother-younger brother*: In the languages of cultures influenced by Confucianism, different terms are used to refer to an older or younger brother. The distinction is important as it not only denotes rank (and status within the family) but an elder brother or older sibling is expected to help raise the younger ones, especially if either of the parents dies while the children are young.

3. *Husband-wife*: Mutual care and responsibility are expected in this relationship but it is nonetheless hierarchical. The husband is expected to be the authoritative protector who takes care of the wife, while the wife is expected to obey and fulfill her role as a mother at home.

4. *Elder-junior*: This covers all forms of relationships that involve one person who is older than another. As the older is deemed to be wiser, he would always be the mentor in the relationship and the younger person must show respect and heed the advice rendered. The implications of this bond extend to teacher-student, employer-employee, expert-apprentice, and even between friends.

5. *Ruler* (benevolence)-*subject* (loyalty): As discussed, all rulers are to reign based on the principle of *ren* and subjects reciprocate through loyalty to the ruler.

Human Flourishing

The ideal of the Noble Man would inherently lead towards the progress of society and community which would in turn bring about the flourishing of humanity. This will be discussed in chapter 6.

CHAPTER 5

Religion of Buddha

A man may be in every way a good man and a true believer, and yet be in a false position.

Gilbert Keith Chesterton

It is easy to forget that Buddhism is not indigenous to China in view of how well it has enculturated into society. Buddhism showed up on Chinese soil around the third century BC, bringing far more than a religion to this otherwise isolated civilization.[1] The arrival of this Indian belief system brought a new way of life and of looking at life. Though some rejected it initially, its appearance in the Chinese context changed the Chinese worldview so gradually and thoroughly that very few realized the assimilation was taking place. As Buddhism dominated the Chinese mind for almost a thousand years, we would not understand how it has shaped the Cultural Chinese's worldview unless we look briefly at the way it came into being, as well as the key areas where it has the most cultural impact.

Though having grown up as a Daoist-Buddhist I knew and understood very little of Buddhism. While I followed my parents to temples and performed certain rituals, I was mostly ignorant of their significance. It was not until I became a Christian when I was a teenager that my interest in Buddhism as a religion was piqued. I wanted to learn what it was about this belief system that has persuaded more than one billion followers worldwide. Soon, I discovered that Buddhism is not merely a belief system or a religion but a worldview that has cultural and social impact. This is especially evident in countries like Thailand, Cambodia, Sri Lanka and China where there has been a long history of Buddhist adherence. For instance, a missionary friend of ours in Cambodia once informed us that there is no word in Khmer that would aptly communicate the idea of "mind." This, we suspect, is a result of the entrenchment of the Buddhist (*Theravada*) doctrine that denies the existence of the soul.

Today, various forms of Buddhism are seeing a resurgence and there is unprecedented growth witnessed even in the West. With the influence of media and popular culture, coupled with celebrity converts like Richard Gere, increasingly more people are attracted to the Buddhist way in everything from personal growth, business practices, to better sex. However, the Buddhism that one encounters in the West is so commercialized and Westernized that Boston University's Stephen Prothero calls this form of Buddhism "Boomer Buddhism," in contrast to traditional Buddhism.[2]

In reality, Buddhism as a belief system, worldview and culture is extremely complex as it has evolved over thousands of years and today exists in countless forms differing in doctrine and practice. It is often believed, especially among those who subscribe to Boomer Buddhism, that Buddhism is a highly tolerant and inclusive religion but this is far from being true. According to the Dalai Lama, liberation or salvation is a state that only Buddhists can accomplish. This kind of nirvana is only explained in Buddhist scriptures and can only be achieved through Buddhist practices.[3] Just like most of the other world religions, it claims to hold exclusive knowledge towards liberation from the miserable state of humanity.

Buddhism emerged as a reform movement within Hinduism and was founded by Siddharta Gautama, a prince of the Sakya clan, more than 2,000 years ago. It is hard to really recount the historical events of Gautama's life because much of what is available has been embellished, hence making it difficult to separate historical fact from legendary fiction.[4]

However, there are some details about Gautama's life that are considered historically credible: born and raised a prince at a time when knowledge of the world was only limited to the people he interacted with, Gautama was deliberately sheltered from the reality beyond the grounds of the palace. As his father had planned for him to take over the throne, he was educated and trained as a warrior. One day, he disobeyed his father and ventured out of the palace and witnessed four scenarios that tormented him: an old man, crooked and toothless; an ill man wasted by disease; a corpse; and an ascetic. These are known as the Famous Four Sights of Buddha.[5] Unable to forget what he encountered, Gautama was plagued by the problem of human suffering and of death. Consequently, he left his family and inheritance behind to pursue answers to the many questions he had about life.

Legend tells us that after a long mental struggle, he experienced insight and enlightenment about life and death — he became the Buddha ("the awakened or enlightened one"). All these happened under the bodhi tree (also known as the tree of enlightenment) while he was seated in a lotus position (hence the symbol of the lotus flower in Buddhism). Having found the answer to the questions that afflicted him, he led his life teaching the way to enlightenment until his death at 80 (circa 480–386 BC). After his death, his followers claimed that he gained *parinirvana* — the state of ultimate enlightenment of which there is no need for rebirth.[6]

Teachings of Buddha

Since Buddha's teachings were passed on orally, it is problematic to know exactly what they were. After several centuries of being passed down orally and being interpreted in a variety of ways, the written versions were recorded. Today, although the expression and the practice of the various forms of Buddhism are so diverse, their core beliefs can still somewhat be summarized in the Three Marks of Reality, the Four Noble Truths and the Noble Eightfold Path.[7]

Three Marks of Reality

These Three Marks of Reality are Buddha's assessment of reality and form the basis for the Four Noble Truths and the Eightfold Path. According to Buddha, reality manifests three characteristics:

1. *Constant change:*

   Buddha held that nothing is permanent in the world. *Annica* (in Pali) is the belief that all of reality and life is in a state of constant change — nothing we experience in life remains the same. The assumption that reality consists of permanent, unchanging entities is illusory.[8] Everything is in constant flux. For example, we are growing old by the second, people experience changes of heart and mind, etc.

2. *Permanent self/identity does not exist:*

   If nothing is permanent, then there cannot be any permanent or enduring self or soul either.[9] As such, Buddha believed that individual selves, too, do not truly exist (*anatta*) and are merely an illusion.[10] If the notion of self is an illusion, when Buddhists speak of rebirth, it is not really the enduring soul that is being reincarnated. Instead, a person or a soul is nothing more than an ever-changing combination of psychophysical forces like matter, sensations, perceptions and so on.[11]

3. *Reality is rife with suffering:*

   In fact, as long as one believes in the illusion that a permanent self or a soul exists, one would be bound to the vicious cycle of rebirth (*samsara*) into suffering. However, realizing *anatta* is key to attaining enlightenment (nirvana). In other words, as soon as one realizes that one does not actually exist, and gives up all desires, one will be liberated from the cycle of rebirth unto enlightenment. Hence, attaining enlightenment is the goal of the Buddhist. However, it is worthy to note here that the varying schools of Buddhism interpret the concept of nirvana and enlightenment differently.

The Four Noble Truths

In view of the three features of reality, Buddha taught that the following are truths that must be recognized. These truths, along with solutions to the human predicament, are succinctly captured by a traditional account of Buddha's first sermon:

> Now this, O monks, is the noble truth of pain: birth is painful, old age is painful, sickness is painful, death is painful, sorrow, lamentation, dejection, and despair are painful. Contact with unpleasant things is painful, not getting what one wishes is painful. In short the five khandas of grasping are painful. Now this, O monks, is the noble truth of the cause of pain: that craving which leads to rebirth, combined with pleasure and lust, finding pleasure here and there, namely craving for passion, the craving for existence, the craving for non-existence. Now this, O monks, is the noble truth of the cessation of pain: the cessation without a remainder of that craving, abandonment, forsaking, release, non-attachment. Now this, O monks, is the noble truth of the way that leads to the cessation of pain: this is the noble Eightfold Path, namely, right views, right attention, right speech, right action, right livelihood, right effort, right mindfulness, right concentration.[12]

1. **Dukkha**: Suffering is universal — life is fundamentally fraught with disappointment, dissatisfaction and discontent of every kind. All of human existence is characterized by suffering. There are many aspects of suffering ranging from all forms of physical and mental pain to changes in circumstances of life, resulting in unhappiness and suffering.

2. **Samudaya**: The cause of suffering — at the root of our suffering is our desires and cravings. Our desires need not be bad to cause us pain. Rather the very state of craving or thirsting for anything at all would result in *dukkha*.

3. **Nirodha**: The end of suffering — when we cease to have cravings, desires and longings, we will be liberated from suffering. Also, when one attains nirvana, that is, to realize one's non-existence, one ceases to suffer.

4. *Mangga*: The liberation from suffering — the way to achieve freedom from our desires and cravings can be found in following the Noble Eightfold Path that will help us end all our dissatisfaction and discontent.

Translated into our contemporary world:
Jon Lee is due for a promotion at his company. With the promotion comes a huge salary raise (desire) that would enable him to buy the car he has always wanted as well as the house (craving) his wife has been looking at. In vying for the position (desire), he has been working 50 hours a week (suffering), resulting in him spending little time with his children and wife. His relationship with them has been rife with misunderstanding and quarrels (suffering). Then his doctor informs him that his medical report shows a problem with his liver (suffering).

The remedy to Jon Lee's predicament is for him to stop desiring and craving all that he is pursuing. After all, his existence is an illusion and since everything is impermanent, his illusive self is also quickly passing into non-existence. Instead, he should focus on following the Noble Eightfold Path to liberate him unto enlightenment.

The Noble Eightfold Path
The Noble Eightfold Path is the Buddhist ethic that calls for principles that fall into three general categories — moral self-discipline, meditation and wisdom:[13]

1. right understanding (involving acceptance of the Four Noble Truths and rejection of incorrect philosophical positions regarding the existence of the self and its destiny, and of unworthy moral attitudes that would lead to greed, lies, etc.);
2. right intention;
3. right speech;
4. right conduct (including charity and abstention from killing any living being);
5. right livelihood;
6. right effort (involving attempts to overcome evil);
7. right mindfulness (of the body, feelings and mental processes); and
8. right concentration (involving taming and controlling of the mind).

The Various Schools of Buddhism

One of the reasons why Buddhism is so complex and diverse is that there are at least two branches of the religion and within them are scores of schools that teach doctrines of differing emphases and often even contradict each other. Theravada Buddhism is the fundamentalist branch of Buddhism as it is believed the traditions of this branch are closest to Buddha's original teachings. This form of Buddhism is atheistic in its orientation as adherents of Theravada Buddhism esteem Buddha as a great teacher or saint but never as a God. This branch holds that Buddhist teachings are reserved only for the monks and that only Buddhist monks can attain nirvana. Lay adherents are only secondary participants in the religion and their goal is to lead a good life to store up enough merit for a better rebirth.

Consequently, the school of Mahayana Buddhism emerged in reaction against the elitism and individualism of early Buddhism. Mahayana Buddhism taught that everyone could have faith in and devotion for the Buddha, and love and compassion for all living beings. In the Lotus Sutra — the definitive scriptures of the Mahayana school — it is declared that Buddha had a new revelation. This new revelation brought about some important departures from Theravada Buddhism.[14]

For one, Buddha's teaching of salvation through works had been too narrow and the new revelation states that, from now, salvation will be bestowed by faith. Also, now all men are called to Buddhahood. These departures from Theravada Buddhism led to the worship of a growing number of divine beings in the form of buddhas and bodhisattvas. These divine figures are esteemed as either saviors or teachers who have the knowledge to lead others toward enlightenment — for example, the appearance of *Avalokita* (Sanskrit) or *Guanyin* in Chinese. Some bodhisattvas have achieved enlightenment but have chosen to delay their nirvana so that they can save those who put their faith in them through the bodhisattvas's accumulated merits.

These developments also gave rise to the founding of new schools of Buddhism that introduced all kinds of new principles and beliefs. For example, Amida Buddhism, Zen Buddhism and Nichiren Buddhism all teach different ideas about the enlightenment (nirvana) and how to achieve it. It is with these liberal doctrines that Buddhism set its mark in China.

Chinese Buddhism

Up until this point in history, Chinese civilization remained mostly isolated from the outside world. But with the advent of Buddhism in China, all this would change. The spread of Buddhism from India did not merely bring a new system of beliefs but introduced a whole new way of life and thinking about the world. The Chinese soul would never be the same again from here on. Creel, in his observation of Chinese thought rightly states, "The whole Chinese manner of thinking was to some extent changed, so gradually and so universally that very few people knew what was happening. For roughly a thousand years the Chinese mind was largely dominated by Buddhism."[15]

There are limited historical records to indicate exactly when and how Buddhism arrived in China but what sets this foreign religion apart from Christianity's propagation in China was the way in which it reached the Chinese. Instead of Indian monks being sent by foreigners into China, it was the Chinese emperor of the Tang dynasty who sought for this non-native faith in the early stages of Buddhism's spread. Traditions tell of the story of Emperor Ming's (AD 63) dream during the Tang dynasty. In his dream, he saw a golden man flying into his palace which was interpreted to be an Indian deity. So the emperor sent an entourage to India and brought back Buddhist scriptures, relics and images on a white horse. The accompanying monks then founded the White Horse monastery in Henan.[16]

While it is possible that Buddhism may have entered China before this via the trade routes, this royal patronage marked its official arrival. However, this did not necessarily pave the way for Buddhism to expand in China because there were many hurdles to this foreign religion taking root. One significant challenge was the difference in their view of the world. The Chinese worldview thus far, as shaped by Daoism and Confucianism, was essentially more pragmatic and secular in nature and mostly concerned with the present life.[17] For example, within Confucianism, the individual self is defined with respect to a collective web of relationships and prescribed duties to family and to society. Meanwhile, the Buddhist idea of no-self, individual liberation and monastic withdrawal contradicted the prescribed social aspirations and seemed foreign to the Chinese temperament. The Buddhist goal was other-worldly oriented (ideas such as nirvana) while Confucius's teachings centered on how to live right in the here and now.

Hence Buddhism had to adopt and assimilate in order to gain acceptance in this foreign culture. It found an ally in the mysticism of Daoism and the two were often associated together. Dialogues and negotiations between Buddhism, Daoism and Confucianism that occurred over the dynasties of Sui, Tang, Wei, Jin, and the dynasties of South and North saw the birth of a school of Buddhism that is indigenous to the Chinese culture — Ch'an Buddhism (Zen Buddhism in Japan).[18]

Ch'an Buddhism adopted a Chinese style and is rather different from the original Buddhism of India. Despite the initial challenges to Buddhism's acceptance in China, there were many compelling reasons for its rapid growth and eventual entrenchment in the Cultural Chinese worldview. For one, Confucius's teachings were seen to be elitist (one needed to read fairly well to truly understand the teachings) and they hardly made any speculation about heaven and spiritual matters (i.e. life after death).

However, in Buddhism, almost everyone has a fair chance of salvation.[19] In addition, that there are compassionate bodhisattvas like *Guanyin* ready to help those in need was a powerful draw to many who recognized their human frailty and weakness. Buddhism was also able to address the human psyche where it provided a systematic explanation of the world and human life that ultimately defines practical life — Buddhahood (i.e. purpose, meaning, etc). As the Buddhist hope of nirvana provided a consolation to many who were suffering in the present world, it was not surprising that the period of tremendous growth of Chinese Buddhism was when the Chinese world was exceedingly troubled in the second century AD.[20]

Neo-Confucianism — The Three in Harmony
The rapid success of Buddhism, however, also caused it to be entangled in various political and economic abuses. Influential monks with access to royal power in the courts who controlled swelling coffers and thought they were exempt from the Buddhist moral code abounded. This tarnished the reputation of Buddhism. Meanwhile, Buddhism's rapid expansion had long concerned the Confucian philosophers.

After the death of Confucius, Confucianism underwent various stages of evolution.[21] First was when Mencius and Xunzi established their respective schools of thought, taking Confucius's teachings in two diverse directions. Next, a variety of pseudo-scientific reasoning and cosmological speculations were grafted into Confucianism. This, as well as the need for reform to counter the invasion of Buddhism, led to the evolution of the third stage of Confucianism — Neo-Confucianism.[22]

During the Sung Dynasty (AD 960–1279), in an attempt to stave off Buddhism, Confucian scholars developed a new basis of explanation of the universe that is as comprehensive as Buddhism's and that allowed for a synthesis of Daoist, Buddhist and Confucian principles and tendencies. In some ways it is a misnomer to name the philosophy Neo-Confucianism as in many of its conceptions, it is more Daoist and Buddhist than Confucianist.[23]

A contemporary example of this is the renowned Tu Weiming who calls himself a New Confucianist (and is part of the Boston Confucians). His view is evidently heavily influenced by the philosophies of Daoism and Buddhism:[24]

> *We are here because embedded in our human nature is the secret code for heaven's self-realization. Heaven is certainly omnipresent, may even be omniscient, but is most likely not omnipotent. It needs our active participation to realize its own truth. We are heaven's partners, indeed co-creators. We serve heaven with common sense, the lack of which nowadays has brought us to the brink of self-destruction. Since we help heaven to realize itself through our self-discovery and self-understanding in day-to-day living, the ultimate meaning of life is found in our ordinary, human existence.*[25]

Today you will rarely find a Cultural Chinese who perceives life purely according to the teachings of Laozi, Confucius or Buddha. However, much of these three philosophies have shaped our worldview and culture. As we examine the traits that describe the Cultural Chinese soul, you will find traces of these philosophies entrenched in their beliefs and perceptions of the world, as well as in their cultural traditions. One such example is the veneration of ancestors.

Qingming: A Case Study in Veneration of the Dead

The traditional Chinese death rite is such that at death, the body is buried and paper models of houses, maids, DVD players, cars and other household items are burnt so that the deceased would have them for their life in hell. A lot of spirit money (also called hell money) is burned so that the deceased will have enough to spend in the afterlife. Regular visits are made to their graves to spring-clean the tomb area and to make similar offerings to the deceased. In the homes of the living, at the family altar, a wooden tablet is placed to represent the deceased's place in the household. On the altar, joss sticks are burnt and, often, food is offered to appease the dead. Sometimes, the living may regard their ancestors as "guardian angels" — protecting them from serious accidents, or guiding their path in life.

Then, after about ten years, the body is dug up and the bones buried again in an auspicious site — this is the *shi gu* rite (literally "pick up bones"). One festival that is synonymous with the practice of veneration of the dead is *Qingming*. *Qingming* day, which also marks the beginning of spring, is focused on ancestral veneration. On this day, family members will visit ancestral graves where special rites are held and offerings made in honor of the ancestors. Such events are related to the Chinese tradition of receiving blessings from previous generations when undertaking a new venture.

Visiting the cemetery is referred to as *hang shan* (walking the mountain). A series of activities — clearing the gravesite of dirt and debris, weeding around the site, and repainting inscriptions on the gravestone — are together referred to as "sweeping" the grave. Wine and a variety of foods may be placed around the gravesite (along with appropriate tableware such as glasses and chopsticks) as offerings to the spirit of the deceased. Eating the food that was offered to the deceased is considered good luck. Paper money is burned for use in the afterlife, candles are lit, and family members bow and kneel in respect. Many of today's offerings may be simple, consisting of incense, paper money and flowers.

As this tradition is steeped in superstition, it is impossible to clearly classify which system of belief has influenced which rite. Instead, the motivation for each rite is a combination of Daoist, Confucian and Buddhist principles with animistic beliefs. This practice of ancestral veneration is ultimately based on the following beliefs about reality:

1. Filial piety is important;
2. the departed can bless or curse their living relatives where a person's good or bad fortune is influenced by the souls of his or her ancestors;
3. all departed ancestors have the same material needs they had when alive; and

4. all departed ancestors would need the help of their living family to help them eventually be reincarnated.

Confucianism: In addition to the influence of the importance of filial piety, Confucius's idea of *Tian Ming* (the Mandate of Heaven) — the belief that heaven knows best and will watch over us — also plays a part in shaping the practice of this tradition. Heaven knows "best" but what is "best" is often defined by material or financial prosperity. Meanwhile, the will of our ancestors is deemed equivalent to the *Tian Ming*. As such, if we are to prosper, we must seek the will and guidance of our ancestors even after they have passed on from this world. This belief in the wisdom of our ancestors also suggests that we are able to communicate with our deceased ancestors.

Buddhism: With the introduction of Buddhism into the Chinese belief system, the idea of reincarnation, accumulation and transference of merit were incorporated into ancestral veneration. Our ancestors are believed to have many reincarnations until they achieve enlightenment. Some of the things one can do to be assured of being reincarnated into a good life are the performance of certain rites. One's descendants can do these in proxy. Therefore, if one truly venerates one's parent, one would perform as many of such rites as possible to ensure that the deceased would be reincarnated well.

Hence, when a Christian child informs a parent that he will not be able to take part in such rituals, he is in actual fact saying that he will not help his parents to escape hell into being reincarnated well. This is seen as a clear violation of filial piety.

Daoism: Daoism introduced a pantheon of deities and immortals into the Chinese belief system. As such, the performance of certain rites for the dead would not only ensure reincarnation into a good life, it may even lead one to be an immortal (*xian*) or deity in heaven.

Shenism: Traditional beliefs about the spirit world contributed the idea of a spirit world that is parallel to our present physical world. In this spirit world, a host of spirits and gods rule and function just like ours. These spirits consist of both demons and gods (*gui* and *shen*). These beings have similar experiences to ours — emotions (hunger, jealousy, anger); needs (marriage, money, housing, etc.); and hence should be treated accordingly.

This tradition of ancestral veneration as observed today is a perfect example of how the beliefs of Daoism, Confucianism and Buddhism have syncretized with animistic beliefs (Shenism) about the world and shaped popular Cultural Chinese practices and rites. This kind of harmonization is not unique to the *Qingming* ceremony. Similar influence can also be detected in other Cultural Chinese customs during Lunar New Year, Mid-autumn Festival (Mooncake Festival), wedding ceremonies and other celebrations.

As we recognize how entrenched the philosophies of Daoism, Confucianism and Buddhism are in the Cultural Chinese worldview, the challenge before us is to present them the truth of a seemingly foreign belief about reality. However, if Christ is the Lord of all nations (Rev. 7:9–10), then the Good News must somehow be relevant to even the Cultural Chinese. We will explore if that is the case by digging deeper into Confucius's ideal.

CHAPTER 6

Confucius's Utopia

The man who in the view of gain thinks of righteousness; who in the view of danger is prepared to give up his life; and who does not forget an old agreement however far back it extends: such a man may be reckoned a complete man.

Analects 9:13

If necessity is the mother of invention, then dissatisfaction must be the father of philosophical ideologies. Buddhism, for example, was founded on the grounds of Siddharta Gautama's dissatisfaction with the Hindu caste system that had contributed to the suffering prevalent around him: Why do we suffer? What causes suffering? What is the solution to the problem of suffering? In his pursuit for an answer to these existential questions, he conceived of a philosophical framework to help him make sense of reality as well as to help him find a solution to the problems that plague humanity.

Likewise, Confucianism emerged in the midst of sociopolitical chaos where military conflicts over power, wealth and land left many in misery and poverty. Confucius was born during the Zhou Dynasty — a dynasty that was established based on the feudal system. A reign based on the feudal system would see the empire divided into many feudal states under the central government. These feudal states were ruled either by princes and dukes who were members of the royal family, or by those who had given outstanding service to the state.[1] The king, on the other hand, was the chief commander and recognized as the Son of Heaven. As the Son of Heaven, it was believed the king was placed on the throne by Heaven and therefore held the heavenly mandate to rule.

While the feudal system worked well initially, the weakened hold of the Zhou kings over the states led many of the individual states to ignore the authority of the kings and fight with one another for a larger share of land, property and power. The power struggle between the states resulted in the disintegration of social order: people endured endless misery and suffering, with families torn apart due to the military clashes. While the poor common people were living a life of little hope and comfort, the morally corrupt lived in the luxury of their power and wealth.[2]

Against a backdrop of such lawlessness and disorder, many thinkers and philosophers sought ways to solve the social and existential problems they were facing. And Confucius was one of them.

Confucius's Utopia: What Confucius's Ideal Reality Looks Like

Confucius was profoundly moved by the state of the world in which he lived and vowed to dedicate his life to bringing reformation to his world. He concluded that the sociopolitical chaos of his days were a result of the abuse of *li* (ritual/propriety) by the rulers. Instead of fulfilling their duties as caretakers of their citizens, they were more preoccupied with their self-interests and employed immoral ways to achieve them. Under the rule of such ruthless men, the common man suffered. These relentless afflictions upon the common man, in turn, suppressed their well-being and advancement.

Confucius believed that if virtues were taught and lived out, social order could be restored and society would function properly again. He was committed to promoting and reinstating the value of moral virtues especially among the ruling class. However, *li* can only be restored when a righteous government is established. And a government is righteous when the ruler and his officials govern virtuously, especially exemplifying the virtue of *ren* (humaneness or kindness) and fulfilling the duties that are expected of their roles according to the Mandate of Heaven.[3]

Even though Confucius's teachings on the virtues and ways of a benevolent government were recognized as central to his legacy, it should not be mistaken that what he taught only concerned ethics and politics because his main interest ultimately lay in the fundamental principles of what it means to be human.[4] For Confucius, a person's ultimate goal is in attaining full humanness, and hence he or she should be devoted to learning how to be truly human.[5] Needless to say, the fundamental principles of being human make up the core pillars of his teachings, like the virtues: *ren* (humaneness/kindness), *yi* (righteousness), *li* (propriety/ritual), *zhi* (wisdom), as well as the duties that entail the five cardinal relationships as discussed in the previous chapter.

Confucius believed that once we get these fundamental principles right, that is, when virtues are taught as well as lived, we will experience harmony in our social relationships; individuals and families, while the state will experience peace and prosperity. Such a utopian society will in turn serve as a conducive environment for self-cultivation.

1. **A government that is benevolent**
    Besides Islam, much more than other faiths or religions (if we so categorize Confucianism), Confucian teachings place significant emphasis on how to improve the political order of the day. However, Confucius's teachings should never be mistaken as merely a political philosophy because a benevolent government is ultimately a means of achieving self-cultivation and universal love.

For Confucius, there is never a dichotomy between matter and mind, body and soul, as well as the private and public. Humanity is wholistic — always existing as one in society striving for physical well-being, for social harmony and for moral and spiritual perfection.[6]

Since Confucius's discontent with the way of the world was prompted by the corruption and exploitation of the political ranks, his ethical convictions began with the need to deal with the perpetrator of the sociopolitical chaos — the rulers and officials in power.

For him, a good government is naturally made up of virtuous rulers or officials who would govern according to moral virtues like kindness, righteousness and wisdom. When such virtues are exemplified in their governing, they rule according to propriety and observe the prescribed rituals to secure for their people a peaceful and proper environment for efforts of self-cultivation.

In fact, a true test of a benevolent government is when it cares for its subjects so well that citizens of other states would wish to come under its jurisdiction.[7] In fact, Mencius often likened the way in which a government rules to parents' responsibility towards their children.

In other words, the progress of a society begins with the cultivation of virtues within the governing ranks — a government of moral persuasion, with leaders who exemplify personal integrity and selfless devotion to their people. This is obviously an observation that is perennially true as we survey the world and note the number of failing states today due to moral corruption of the government. The consequences of morally depraved officials in power are many, but the most grievous would be the suffering of citizens of the state and their inability to flourish and advance.

Mencius taught that the people of a nation come first while the ruler comes last: "The people are the most important element in a nation; the spirits of the land and grain are the next; the sovereign is the lightest." (Mencius 7B:14) Since it is believed that political power is accorded by the authority of Heaven

(Mandate of Heaven), any government which rules tyrannically will be stripped of this mandate.[8]

Sinologist Julia Ching argues that there are two sides to the coin of this Confucian emphasis on political responsibility. While it may keep tradition alive and relevant, it can (and has) also led to negative consequences of manipulation by the political establishment for its own interest. In such contexts, according to Mencius, the removal of the mandate (of Heaven) from the grasp of the tyrant via a revolution is legitimate (Mencius 1B:8). Hence, the Confucian ideal is when social responsibility complements political responsibility by safeguarding against political tyranny.

2. **A society of self-cultivating Noble Men (and Women)**
    A society that is both socially and politically responsible ought to be populated by those who demonstrate the right moral qualities and virtues. Confucius believed that Noble Men are not simply born but made. Especially with regards to the ruling class, he was very determined to differentiate the Noble Man from those who are simply of noble birth. A person does not qualify as a Noble Man just because he is of the royal family or of the ruling class, as nobility comes from the mind and spirit of a person and not heritage and ancestry.[9]

    A Noble Man is also one who is able to think for himself. Throughout his life, Confucius was willing to help and to teach his students how to think, but they had to find the answers for themselves. He readily admitted that he himself did not know the truth, but only a way to look for it.[10]

    The Confucian pursuit was also not about being a holy person but rather about one who is always open to everything good, true, and beautiful (books, music, art), and one who is committed to his or her social and political responsibilities. This somewhat anthropocentric vision was perhaps what led many to consider Confucianism a secular philosophy instead of a religious system.[11]

    While Confucius held on to the ancient notion of the Heavenly Mandate and there are evidences in the Classics that Confucius himself believed in a personal God, he was not explicit in his teachings about the existence of the divine or about life after death. As such, when it came to the problem of evil, his observation was that it had to be solved by means of moral self-cultivation and righteous politics.[12]

In order for us to grasp Confucius's idea of the cultivation of a Noble Man, it is important for us to examine Confucians' understanding of human nature because the system of ethics and most of the philosophy are based upon that belief. But this is where it gets a little tricky because the Confucian belief about human nature also depends on the category of Confucians. This applies, too, to Confucians' varying (and sometimes contradictory) conceptions of God. According to professor of world cultures, Paulos Huang, there are at least five categories of Confucianisms to consider, including Ancient Confucianism (tradition based on the Classics), Neo-Confucianism (referring to developments during the Tang, Song, Ming and Qing dynasties from the tenth to the nineteenth century), to present-day Modern Confucianism, referring to the third generation (since 1980) of Neo-Confucians.[13]

The Chinese word for human nature (xing) is a compound character of the characters for mind and heart, and life or offspring. Symbolically understood, the human being is one who has received from Heaven the gift of life and all the inherent traits of human nature, especially the ability of moral discernment.[14]

For example, when confronted by a heinous crime, it is common to hear Cultural Chinese exclaim how the perpetrator lacks xing because it is xing that differentiates us from beasts that possess no moral faculty. Therefore it is not surprising that Mencius's belief about the goodness of human nature is most widely accepted — that is, we all possess an intuitive sense of what is right and wrong without having been taught, and we are naturally inclined towards what is good and right. He believed what distinguishes humans from other beings is humanity's sense of right and wrong (Mencius 2A:6).

It is common to hear Cultural Chinese comment on how a guilty person is naturally good but is led astray by bad influences. While the presence of evil is admitted, it is explained away as the product of contact between an originally good human nature and its wicked environment. In other words, evil is seen as a perversion or a deviation of the natural good: "If men do what is not good, the blame cannot be imputed to their natural powers."[15] (Mencius 6A:6)

In addition, the Chinese language does not have a term that is equivalent to the concept of "sin". The nearest is *zui* which is typically used to refer to "crime" — a term that describes an external behavior or an act rather than an internal orientation of the heart and mind. Since we are naturally endowed with innate virtuous inclinations, then given the proper circumstances these virtues can be awakened, cultivated and developed.[16] When we start living a life of virtue, we are simply embodying our true nature. Put simply, a person who is involved in self-cultivation is merely realizing his full humanness.[17]

Though Xunzi believed the opposite about human nature — where humans are inherently evil — both were convinced by Confucius's conviction that human goodness can be cultivated. Self-cultivation is a main concern for Confucian thinkers. Simply defined, self-cultivation is the process where one intentionally acts on shaping one's character according to a certain presumed ethical or moral standard.[18] I remember my mother suggesting that I go to church with my uncle when I was a child so that I would learn how to "be human". Of course, being human in this case was to develop a sense of moral discernment.

Our environment plays a significant role in shaping us morally — a bad environment can ruin our good nature, while a good one is beneficial for our moral cultivation. According to Mencius, studying classical texts written by the sages as well as friendships with other Noble Men are all steps one can take towards becoming Noble Men ourselves. That is why Confucius recognized that he was not merely passing on his wisdom to his followers but was educating them, helping them to develop morally and mentally. In addition, even though the environment was crucial to self-cultivation, a person must also have the desire to achieve this. Other than being negative social influences, immorality or evil actions are also the consequence of our failure to actively train the "greater part of ourselves" (our inclination towards goodness). When we develop the greater part of ourselves, we would be able to prevent our lesser part from indulging in sensual desires and unethical behavior.[19] Confucians believe that we have the ability to orient our desires and attention towards that which is good and virtuous, and act accordingly.[20]

So, how does one become a Noble Man? As discussed in the previous chapter, education coupled with the practice of the two key Confucian moral virtues of kindness and rituals will help one achieve the aspiration of being a Noble Man. However, the practice of rituals is not to be mistaken for a legalistic adherence to a list of do's and don'ts. Rather, the significance of rituals lies in what the practice does to the inner person and not necessarily to their external observances. Hence, without the right inner dispositions, morality becomes mere hypocrisy and legalism (Analects 15:17).[21]

It is interesting to compare Confucius's idea of rituals with the Christian practice of spiritual discipline (like Bible study, fasting, and acts of charity) because both can easily slip into the pitfall of legalism if merely approached from an observable and behavioral perspective.

However, from an early Confucian perspective, one's concern for oneself and for others are integrated in such a way that emphasis on self-cultivation would not lead to the kind of individualism or legalism that some have found concerning.[22] The Confucian vision was always one of a society consisting of individuals who have the qualities of "sageliness within and kingliness without" — the heart of a sage, and the wisdom of a king must be pursued.[23]

Confucius never thought that an individual could exist apart from being in community, but neither did he think of society as being of a higher priority to the individual, such that the identity of the individual is subsumed. Confucius understood that humans are ultimately social beings and their identity is, to a large extent, shaped by the society they are in. Meanwhile since society is essentially the interaction of individuals, the ones who compose it also determine the characteristics of a society.[24]

3. **A society of harmonious relationships conducive to human flourishing**

The end of the Confucian pursuit of the Noble Man (via education, practice of virtues) is not simply political responsibility but the attainment of what it means to be human. This means, it must also entail the discovery of individuals' moral values and inner worth.[25] Confucius believed that individuals could only achieve all of that as a harmonious community of free men and not as isolated individuals.[26] This idea of self-cultivation in community is another distinction between Confucianism and its other competing philosophies like Daoism and Buddhism which advocate lifestyles of solitude and contemplation.

What does Confucius mean by self-cultivation in community? It simply means that learning to become fully human calls for a harmony of the two dimensions of self and others.[27] Self-cultivation must be a socially shared effort because it concerns the ties between the individual and his social relationships. The self is viewed as the center of a web or network of connections of family, friends, colleagues, society and state where these connections all play a part in defining the self. In other words, the self is shaped by the interaction between the individual self and the social self.[28] An individual's identity and life are defined by his or her existence in community.

In fact, it is arguable that the perennial relevance of Confucian teachings lies in how individuals derive their identity, moral self and life purpose from their social relations. This assumes that one's relationship to others in a society is based on mutual benevolence and propriety. These Confucian values of benevolence and propriety are fundamental for a true sense of human dignity, freedom and equality.[29] If there is discord or loss in those relationships, a person's identity is naturally threatened and life may lose its significance. Hence, the harmony of relationships is to be pursued and preserved at all cost.

Harmonious relationships are achieved when those relationships are bound by the Confucian virtues of benevolence and propriety. The moral character of relationships in community can be realized when all live by the principle of reciprocity and kindness which is also known as the Doctrine of Mean or Confucius's Golden Mean:

> To regard everyone as a very important guest, to manage the people as one would assist at a sacrifice, not to do to others what you would not have them do to you. (Analects 15:23)[30]

As the natural family is the most fundamental of all social relationships, the nature of our familial relationships serves as a model for our social behavior — respect your own elders, as well as others' elders; be kind to your own children and juniors, as well as those of others. The relationships of a natural family are seen as an ideal that ought to guide all other relationships. This is where the Confucian society views itself as one big family: "Within the four seas all men are brothers." (Analects 12:5) The duties following from these relationships are mutual and reciprocal — for example, a subject owes loyalty to his ruler just like a child owes respect to his or her parents.[31]

An everyday example of this is how Cultural Chinese address those who are not related to us as if they are family. When my husband first moved to Asia, he was perplexed by how I would address strangers that I interact with — like taxidrivers and storekeepers — as Uncle or Aunty. This is second nature to most of us Cultural Chinese and we would never stop to think why we would *not* do so. This is a cultural ritual practiced to show respect to anyone who is older than us. Sometimes this is even extended to those who are younger than us where we address them as "Little/Younger Brother" or "Little Sister."

Upon understanding the value of this cultural practice, my husband started addressing others in the same way, too. I found out later that it solved a Jackie Chan movie mystery for him: when he used to watch those movies (dubbed literally in English), he used to wonder how it was that the characters in the movies had such big families, because Jacky Chan would address everyone as either Uncle, Aunty, Brother or Sister.

Now he realizes that not all of them were family but that the references were simply respectful ways of addressing others. It also did not take long for my husband to start addressing taxidrivers as Uncles, sometimes to the chagrin of those who were obviously younger than him.

The definition of Confucius's virtue of benevolence is broader than just kindness. It is associated with the notion of loyalty and reciprocity (Analects 4:15) and is a virtue that is rooted in human sentiments of love, respect and affection. It is ultimately a fundamental orientation of life towards others that motivates us in our practice of rituals.[32]

As discussed in the previous chapter, Confucius's sense of rituals is essentially the guiding principle on how we ought to conduct our daily life — from manners to behavior in all social situations. There is a proper way for everyone, in their specific roles in society, to carry themselves in every situation. So, when everyone practices benevolence and propriety and behaves civilly towards each other, the natural outcome would be a society of harmonious relationships that enables us to focus on pursuing happiness, prosperity and progress. In other words, when we take moral corruption and social conflict out of the equation, we will have a social space that fosters well-being, progress and prosperity.

The Confucian vision for an ideal society is then very straightforward — the only way for a society to experience peace and to flourish was to be one that consists of Noble Men that live harmoniously with each other. It is a civil society where all know their place and live out their social responsibilities accordingly.

Put simply, this is the virtuous cycle of the Confucian utopia where self-cultivating Noble Men govern virtuously (political responsibility) so that the community can live out their social roles according to the prescribed Confucian virtues, which in turn create a harmonious and peaceful society that is conducive for the progress, flourishing and continual self-cultivation of men and women towards becoming Noble Men and Women. However, the question remains as to whether this virtuous cycle really works as it is expected to.

CHAPTER 7

Yahweh's Shalom

I must keep alive in myself the desire for my true country, which I shall not find till after death; I must never let it get snowed under or turned aside; I must make it the main object of life to press on to that country and to help others to do the same.

C.S. Lewis

Not many of us wake up in the morning and exclaim with Louis Armstrong, "What a wonderful world!" Perhaps, this might occasionally happen, such as on the day after one's wedding, or when one has had a baby, or a promotion at work. But soon enough we are hit by the daily annoyances that life brings: the rude lady who cuts into your line or the bank statement about charges for a service you did not ask for. Then there are regrets: a range of regrets from having bought into a deceptive business scheme, to having neglected a family member or friend until it was too late when he died of cancer.

There is also the problem of aging. When I asked my son to wish my father "Happy Birthday" when he turned 70, the then seven-year-old asked why we celebrated birthdays. Puzzled by such a question, I asked him "Why not?" to which he responded, "Well, with every birthday we are closer to our death. So, why would we celebrate that?" Great point, because which of us relishes the fact that we are growing older by the second? In fact, it frustrates me that my old eyes need reading glasses and that I need to color my hair every four weeks. Which of us would not feel the remorse in our soul as we recognize that time is passing and carrying with it opportunities and experiences that will not come again?[1]

Everyone experiences loneliness — some more often than others — even if you are married or surrounded by loved ones. It is like an undeniable but indescribable sense of homesickness — for something, someone or somewhere. Closely linked to this is the experience of *ennui*, a wearying boredom. "Mommy, I'm bored!" — an oft-stated complaint in my household by my eight-year-old as he slowly familiarizes with this universal ache of the soul. Soon enough, he will discover that nothing this world has to offer will satiate this *ennui* cavity.

I can go on but suffice to say the whole array of human miseries — from restlessness and estrangement through shame and guilt to the insecurities of daily life — all tell us that human life is not as it ought to be.[2] Something is not right. Something is amiss.

When we read the first book of the Bible, God's story opens dramatically. The first five days saw the Master Designer at work — out of nothing, he designed and made light, the universe, sun, moon, stars; then on the earth, the sky, the sea, and sea and sky creatures. His creative activities went on until the first male and female were brought into being and given their human responsibilities. And God thought that it was very good and rested (Gen. 1:31).

The creation narrative informs us of how all of creation has been designed and created by God to work and live in a divinely appointed way. The account of creation also affirms the goodness of God's creation. It was a world where there was contentment (Gen. 2:22) as the first pair of humans fulfilled their vocation (Gen. 1:15–20) and were in perfect fellowship with their Creator and Lord (Gen. 3:8–10).

However, the world as we know it is not quite as described in the creation account. In fact, what we experience of reality is contrary to all that is described. If we take a quick survey, how many in our midst would truly say they are secure and content with their life? Instead, many would admit that they wished things were different because their life and the world, in general, are not what they believe they ought to be. We have a desire for a world in which things are as they ought to be and we long for that world.

Some of us may even have a vision for how that ideal world should look like:[3] it would be a world where marriages are resilient and enduring. Families would stay together — there would not be single parents. Hence children would be secure and loved. Cultural, racial and national diversity would be valued and cherished. There would be no such thing as a caste system. Nor would there be power struggles between the sexes and between the generations. Elected officials would act responsibly to serve the ones they govern. Politicians would tell the truth. One would not need to pay a bribe to have civil applications approved. Criminals would be caught and prosecuted fairly. At work, colleagues would rejoice in one another's promotions. Bosses would be generous, understanding and kind. In short, it would be a world ruled by kindness, peace, justice and trust. It would be a world of generosity and not of scarcity.

This is not surprising because at the core of the biblical understanding of reality is a concept of the way things are supposed to be. The prophets of the Old Testament recognized this as *shalom* — the reality as God had designed and purposed, embodying peace, justice, mutual respect and deliberate consideration of the good of others.[4]

While we may typically understand *shalom* to mean peace and harmony, biblical *shalom* is really much more profound and extensive than that.

Cornelius Plantinga, Jr. puts it beautifully in his book, *Not The Way It's Supposed to Be: A Breviary of Sin*:

> *The webbing together of God, humans, and all creation in justice, fulfillment, and delight is what the Hebrew prophets call shalom....In the Bible, shalom means universal flourishing, wholeness, and delight — a rich state of affairs in which natural needs are satisfied and natural gifts fruitfully employed, a state of affairs that inspires joyful wonder as its Creator and Savior opens the doors and welcomes the creatures in whom he delights. Shalom, in other words, is the way things ought to be.*[5]

This shalomic reality is all-encompassing and wholistic where it concerns the relationship of not just the individual and his or her community, but the persons of the Trinitarian God, the physical world, as well as between particular communities or societies, where each entity would have its own wholeness while also possessing many edifying relations to other entities. *Shalom* is being in a state of wholeness on the spiritual, personal and social dimensions, thus resulting in a rich and flourishing existence. It is God's supreme will for humanity and humanity's calling.

We see the birth of such a world in the first few chapters of Genesis. However, the cosmic tragedy of the fall of humanity disrupted its full actualization. Sadly, despite their shalomic paradise, the first couple were deluded into believing that they could be their own god. Genesis 3 records the entrance of sin where the first humans chose to act against God's command and believed in the lie of Satan. They rejected their nature as created, limited and finite beings, and tried to be what they could never be — divine. In other words, they wanted to be their own god. In willfully believing in the lie of the Enemy, they have betrayed their Creator and vandalized *shalom*.

Hence, sin is not merely the breaking of rules. It is a state of rebellion against God and his purposes. Our severed relationship with God was not the only consequence of sin. Our state of death resulted in broken relationships at all levels and affects all of life. Insecurities, low self-esteem are among the repercussions of our having rejected the self that God had created us to be.

Sin also alienates us from each other — Adam immediately blamed Eve. And Eve blamed the serpent. And the blaming game has not stopped since. The bitterness, pride and self-centeredness that existed on that day in the Garden of Eden still exist today. Our relationships with the people around us have been tainted by either distrust or obsession.

God created a world where each part intricately depended on or was related to others. Sin disrupted that harmony. All that was created good by God has now been corrupted by sin — for example, sexuality is good but is often distorted by lust and licentiousness. Plantinga Jr. believes that that is why God hates sin — because it violates his law but, more substantively, because it violates *shalom*; it breaks the peace, it interferes with the way things are supposed to be.[6]

However, just because *shalom* has been ruined for now, it does not mean that God has given up on having his purpose fulfilled. Precisely because *shalom* is God's will, it will remain an enduring vision that is consistently promised through the prophets:

> *I will make with them a covenant of peace and banish wild beasts from the land, so that they may dwell securely in the wilderness and sleep in the woods. And I will make them and the places all around my hill a blessing, and I will send down the showers in their season; they shall be showers of blessing. And the trees of the field shall yield their fruit, and the earth shall yield its increase, and they shall be secure in their land. And they shall know that I am the LORD, when I break the bars of their yoke, and deliver them from the hand of those who enslaved them. They shall no more be a prey to the nations, nor shall the beasts of the land devour them. They shall dwell securely, and none shall make them afraid. And I will provide for them renowned plantations so that they shall no more be consumed with hunger in the land, and no longer suffer the reproach of the nations. (Ezek. 34:25–29)*

In the Old Testament we see the vision of *shalom* articulated throughout the history of the Jews. A most familiar proclamation of this vision was by Isaiah when he prophesied to Judah a world where *shalom* prevails and there is peace with God, with self, with fellow humans and with nature:

> *The wolf shall dwell with the lamb, and the leopard shall lie down with the young goat, and the calf and the lion and the fattened calf together; and a little child shall lead them. The cow and the bear shall*

graze; their young shall lie down together; and the lion shall eat straw like the ox. The nursing child shall play over the hole of the cobra, and the weaned child shall put his hand on the adder's den. They shall not hurt or destroy in all my holy mountain; for the earth shall be full of the knowledge of the LORD as the waters cover the sea. (Isa. 11:6–9)

Wolves, leopards and lions are predatory animals. It does not take much imagination to conclude that none would be left of the young goat or fattened calf in their presence.

And in what kind of a world could babies play on cobra's ground and reach into the venomous adder's nest without being harmed? It probably would not be a stretch to add that in this fairy-tale world there would not be any division or war. But the prophetic visions are not a fantasy because *shalom* is humanity dwelling at peace in all their relationships: with God, with self, with each other and with nature. The prophet Hosea proclaims a similar vision to Israel:

And I will make for them a covenant on that day with the beasts of the field, the birds of the heavens, and the creeping things of the ground. And I will abolish the bow, the sword, and war from the land, and I will make you lie down in safety. (Hos. 2:18)

Though *shalom* was first articulated in the Old Testament, we see its greater expression and revelation in the New Testament. Old Testament theologian Albert H. Baylis believes that since creation was marred by sin, for *shalom* to come to pass the existing reality must yield to a new creation that will bear the characteristics conducive for *shalom*. In that sense, he adds, God's act of creation did not end in Genesis but continues to develop as we journey to its fulfillment in the person of Christ.[7]

Yahweh's *shalom* could not materialize under fallen humanity but, through Jesus, God will bring his plan to pass. First in the incarnation (along with the crucifixion and resurrection of the Messiah), and subsequently through the life of the Church, we see the divine Son of God enter into our messy sin-infected world so that he can usher in the era of the new creation. In fact, we can even go so far as to say that the promised Messiah, the Christ, *is* the embodiment of *shalom*. The Gospel accounts tell us of how Christ advances *shalom* by healing the sick (Mark 1:40–42, Luke 7:18–23), setting the oppressed free (Mark 5:1–20) and ultimately forgiving sins to bring hope and new life. Repentance, forgiveness, redemption, reconciliation and restoration are all part of humanity's journey towards *shalom*.

Furthermore, Christ did not only embody *shalom*, he empowered his people toward that vision and the Church is now tasked with the mission of spreading the good news of God's will for humanity. Hence, the new creation is not simply a reboot of the original one, but an improved creation where sin and death are done away with for good.

Biblical *Shalom*: Reality as God Intended

Even though this extraordinary vision of well-being, harmony and human flourishing is comprehensive in its scope and reach, and an extensive separate discussion would be necessary to spell out its many dimensions and diverse nuances, we can see three main themes recurring when it comes to the nature of biblical *shalom*.

1. **Harmonious and delightful relationship with God**

   If *shalom* is the supreme will of Yahweh, then we cannot understand it apart from a reference to God. The creation account tells us that unlike other creatures, humans are created in the image of the Trinitarian God. As divine image-bearers we are created specifically for personal relationships with God. We bear the privilege of relating to God in a way that is different from animals. We reflect God and belong to him in a way that is different from other creatures. Therefore when the first humans desired to "be like God," they essentially had stooped down to the lordship of one that is inferior to the God that they belonged to and were meant to worship. Today, though many of us may not literally bow to idols, things of our own design control us — our desires, ambitions, addictions, and false securities.

   As *shalom* begins with being in a right relationship with God, it is then God's design for creation as well as for the redemption. *Shalom* in the Garden of Eden was lost because Adam and Eve believed the enemy and betrayed the trust of Yahweh. The principal relationship that is the lifeline of a flourishing life is the one with the Creator. Hence, the reinstatement of *shalom* must begin with the restoration of humanity's relationship with God. Sin and death, which stand between humanity and

God, must be dealt with effectively for the vision of *shalom* to come true. And it is for this purpose that the last Adam came to fulfill.

Many have come to believe that the message of the gospel is merely about the salvation of our souls. This is a ghastly mistake reinforced by our contemporary consumerist worldview. Yes, the gospel is about our salvation but it is so much more than that. The heart of the gospel is *shalom* — the fulfillment of God's plan and purpose for all of creation. That is why the author of Romans writes:

> *For the creation waits with eager longing for the revealing of the sons of God. For the creation was subjected to futility, not willingly, but because of him who subjected it, in hope that the creation itself will be set free from its bondage to corruption and obtain the freedom of the glory of the children of God. For we know that the whole creation has been groaning together in the pains of childbirth until now. And not only the creation, but we ourselves, who have the firstfruits of the Spirit, groan inwardly as we wait eagerly for adoption as sons, the redemption of our bodies. For in this hope we were saved.* (Rom. 8:19–24a)

Shalom must begin with a right relationship with God where we no longer flee from him like the first humans did in the Garden of Eden. Our recognition of his lordship and kingship also involves worship, holiness, obedience and service.[8] This harmonious relationship with God sees humanity delighting in God and finding great pleasure and fulfillment in our service to him. We look to him as the source of our joy, purpose and are passionate about our fellowship with him. *Shalom* is perfected when humanity recognizes that in its service of God is true happiness.[9]

2. **Harmonious and delightful relationship with each other**
    In addition to a thriving relationship with God, *shalom* is also characterized by harmonious social relationships and delight in the human community. *Shalom* can never be present in a society that is merely a collection of individuals doing life in isolation from each other. *Shalom* is not simply the absence of hostility,

nor merely being in right relationship with each other. Just like how delight in our relationship with God and in service to him is essential to *shalom*, enjoyment of our social relationships is also vital to the advent of *shalom*. To dwell in *shalom* is to enjoy living before God and to enjoy living with one's fellows. Some may even add that it is also to live in harmony with oneself and with nature.[10] These were certainly all part of the prophetic vision the Old Testament prophets had — a time when Yahweh would make things right again — when God's people would work in peace and productively, when humanity would relate to each other like a family and, together with all of creation, we would be under the charge and care of God.[11]

Scripture reveals to us that God is not a force but a person. God is a personal being who involves himself with his creation and relates to it. He is also the unique divine being who exists as three distinct persons — God is one divine substance who exists uniquely as three distinct persons. This implies that before the creation of man, God already experienced fellowship within himself — the Father, the Son and the Holy Sprit were in perfect fellowship and in love with each other (John 1:1–2; 17:5, 24; 10:30). And humans do not just reflect their Creator by way of possessing intelligence, creativity and morality, they also reflect the Trinitarian God socially. We are social beings and we only flourish in relationship with God and with each other. (This is one reason why social isolation via imprisonment is an apt punishment for crime.)

Every month, my family and two other families meet for a home-cooked meal and afterwards discuss life, work and parenting while our children play and have their own activities. We belong to different churches and have very different vocations but this informal fellowship has been an intentional effort to foster spiritual friendship in a fallen world that is increasingly fragmented. As we fellowship over bowls of steamed rice, we experience a foretaste of this *shalom*. The children in the group, especially the boys, look forward to this monthly social because, I suspect, they, too, have tasted the sweetness of *shalom*.

In many of the imageries of *shalom* in the Old Testament, we see peace is always associated with justice. Hence, a key characteristic of shalomic social relationships is justice.[12] If *shalom* encompasses right relationships with each other, then there is no place for exploitation of the disadvantaged or oppression of the weak.[13] The belief that all humans are made in the image of the Trinitarian God serves as the basis for us to simultaneously affirm the unity and diversity of the human race. Right relationships are expressed in love and respect for one another as people created in the image of the divine. This includes committing one's self to the good of the other despite our flaws and brokenness. Hence, a community where *shalom* exists is one where we perform our duties to God as well as to one another.

However, *shalom* is more than that. It is fully present only when there is harmony as well as delight in our relationships and not merely a fulfilling of our obligations.[14] This vision of wholeness is one in which we are not bound only to God but to one another in a caring, sharing, rejoicing community.[15]

We live right by a church that has always impressed me by their sense of community. Every Sunday after their worship service, families would gather at the dining hall to actually *share* their meals. While the adults caught up over lunch, the children would enjoy their time playing with each other. It felt like a big family gathered for a celebration — the atmosphere of the fellowship was filled with hospitality, warmth and gladness. And, despite the large size of the church, everyone seemed to know each other. Everyone was family.

One day, I witnessed an incident that deeply questioned my impression of this church community: one of the church members arriving for service accidentally knocked a cyclist off his bicycle. It was clearly the driver's fault, but instead of stopping to find out how the victim was, the driver parked his car and walked off as if nothing had happened. He could not be bothered. The poor victim sustained minor injuries but was bleeding and in shock. Nobody from the church community came to his help either. He had to call his friends who came to his aid and eventually called the police. The callous disregard of the driver presented to me a major flaw of the fellowship of the community in question — while there was a great sense of unity and love within that community, there seemed to be a lack of even civility, let alone love, for those who were outside.

It appeared that what this community had was perhaps not true *shalom* but mere camaraderie, because the right relationships that are the basis of *shalom* involve more than harmony and delight within our own community but also with those who are without.

Our rebellion that violated *shalom* is both individual and corporate. As individuals we have turned against God. Corporately we have consciously or unconsciously created social and cultural systems that perpetuate the disruption of *shalom*.[16] The parable of the Good Samaritan points out to us that we must extend our hand of fellowship beyond our comfort zone and beyond our convenience. Our wounded *shalom* can only heal if we stand up against racism, sexism and other forms of discrimination that obstruct the cultivation of harmonious and delightful relationships.

3. **Harmonious community that flourishes**
Harmony and delight in our relationship with the divine, lived out in a caring, sharing and joyous community, will naturally lead us to the flourishing life that God had intended for his creation.[17] It is the kind of abundant life as promised by Christ (John 10:10) that results from a life of right relationship with him and those in the Body. *Shalom* comes when we are able to exercise our gifts and talents in our work, find fulfillment in our labor and delight in its fruitful results.

After Adam was formed and placed in the Garden, he was charged to "watch over it" (Gen. 2:15). Paradise was not without work and Adam did not just sit around and merely enjoy the fruits in the Garden. Instead, Adam was charged to care for the lower creation. He was asked to name the animals. Humanity was to have dominion over all creation as a result of bearing God's image. Adam and Eve were the representatives of God in stewarding creation. The command to be fruitful and multiply implies that humans are to continue the creative work of God as they go on to create and produce — not *ex nihilo* (from nothing) but from the provisions and resources that are now made available to them.

Contrary to what some may think, work is not the result of sin. Adam and Eve worked before the fall and their work must have been inherently fulfilling and productive. Work was intended to be inspiring and meaningful, just as God appreciated and enjoyed the work of his hands. But work has become difficult and laborious as a result of sin:

> And to Adam he said,
> > "Because you have listened to the voice of your wife
> > > and have eaten of the tree
> > of which I commanded you,
> > > 'You shall not eat of it,'
> > cursed is the ground because of you;
> > > in pain you shall eat of it all the days of your life;
> > thorns and thistles it shall bring forth for you;
> > > and you shall eat the plants of the field.
> > By the sweat of your face
> > > you shall eat bread,
> > till you return to the ground,
> > > for out of it you were taken;
> > for you are dust,
> > > and to dust you shall return." (Gen. 3:17–19)

Today, few would honestly believe that their work in itself, beyond the paycheck, is fulfilling and fruitful. Instead, many suffer from the anxiety of finding no security, no significance, no meaning, no significant purpose in the world and in their work specifically. Many of us work hard because the desire for material goods — that falsely promise happiness and contentment — enslaves us. The belief that anything independent of God can bring us any ultimate fulfillment could not be further from the truth. When we severed our relationship with the one who created us, we also lost the meaning and purpose for which we were intended to live.

However, when that fundamental separation from God is restored, we will get back on the path toward *shalom* — we will be reconciled to each other, regain our calling and mission, and begin to live the flourishing life that God had willed for his people. In our shalomic state, not only will we regain all these, we will be inspired towards meaningful and enjoyable work, and take pride in the results of our labor.

Put simply, *shalom* is the state of reality that God, in his love, richness and generosity, had intended. This state of affairs is characterized by harmony, love, delight, contentment, justice, fruitfulness and all other qualities that enable God's will and purpose to come to pass. Unfortunately, humanity chose to live apart from God and hence vandalized *shalom*. However, God in his patience and goodness promises humanity a return to *shalom*. This began with the incarnation of the Son of God. The homecoming to *shalom* has begun and humanity is on a path that anticipates and leads toward this vision.[18]

CHAPTER 8

Jesus: The Noble Path to Human Flourishing

I am the way, and the truth, and the life.
No one comes to the Father except through me.

Jesus the Christ

The late human rights activist and Nobel Peace Prize laureate, Liu Xiaobo, before he was arrested in 1989, stated the following in his speech:

> *The Chinese believe that they themselves are the center of the world, and that human beings are omnipotent. But to be omnipotent is actually to be impotent, as the human being is (really) limited. Whether physically or spiritually, the human being is not the center of the world... the tragedy of the Chinese is the tragedy of not having a God. Because of a lack of light from beyond, the darkness on this shore has been mistaken as light...* [1]

Even though Liu's observation was of the sociopolitical soul of the Chinese in China, there is a lot of truth when applied to Cultural Chinese in general. While most Cultural Chinese believe in the goodness of human nature and that we are naturally inclined toward what is good and right, experiences of human nature in reality have exposed the inadequacy of this belief as well as the failure of the Confucian project for human ideals. In the last few years, stories and video clips that show the disturbing and inhumane side of humanity have emerged and gone viral.

As I write this, the latest incident was in Henan province, where a woman who was hit unconscious by a car was ignored by passersby along a busy road, only to be rolled over by an SUV which eventually killed her.[2] The indifference of the people around the victim to her plight was widely denounced. But some were also quick to point out that the inhumanity witnessed was a result of others who took advantage of the kindness of strangers — incidents of people hurling themselves in front of passing vehicles to fake being hit in order to claim damages is becoming the bane of motorists in China.

The 2008 baby formula scandal in China is still fresh in our memory for most of us here in Asia.[3] It was found that powdered infant formula made by large dairy producers there was contaminated by melamine and had caused death and sickness to thousands of babies across China. Apparently melamine was added to diluted milk to boost the protein concentration and hence reap greater profit. It is a tragic commentary of greed, where young, innocent lives were disregarded in an effort to bolster the profit margin.

Here we recall Mencius's optimistic view of human nature and how self-cultivation would actualize true humanness in each of us. However, after so many centuries of striving towards the ideal of the Noble Man and human flourishing, we are not making the kind of progress we had hoped for. Though many Cultural Chinese have progressed financially, morality and civility seem to be on the decline. This is especially true in China where the society is plagued by environmental pollution, widespread corruption, income disparity and the collapse of civility.[4] In fact, social commentator and author, Yu Hua, reports that some in China are longing for a return to the era of Mao Zedong out of nostalgia:

> Although life in the Mao era was impoverished and restrictive, there was no widespread, cruel competition to survive, just empty class struggle, for actually there were no classes to speak of in those days and so struggle mostly took the form of sloganeering and not much else. People then were on an equal level, all alike in their frugal lifestyles; as long as you didn't stick your neck out, you could get through life quite uneventfully. China today is a completely different story. So intense is the competition and so unbearable the pressure that, for many Chinese, survival is like war itself. In this social environment the strong prey on the weak, people enrich themselves through brute force and deception, and the meek and humble suffer while the bold and unscrupulous flourish.[5]

Pastor An, a local pastor in China, believes that the only solution to the self-centeredness that is so prevalent in Chinese society is a higher righteousness that transcends the disengaged self-righteousness.[6] Despite their optimism regarding the goodness of human nature, most Cultural Chinese would concede that humanity does seem to possess weaknesses that make it impossible for us to reach our aspiration of the Noble Man. Mencius, who had a highly optimistic view of man, believed that education and the practice of virtues will bring out the moral and civil self in each of us.

However, the weaknesses of both Cultural Chinese society and culture today seem to indicate that education and the practice of virtues are insufficient as a remedy to the human condition. Someone once quipped that today we run our lives faster and easier but we are running directionless. Nor is there a finish line. Self-cultivation has not been able to adequately bring about the collective human flourishing we hoped for because the basic human predicament seems to be our incapacity for endeavors of the kind — the Christian Scripture tells us the truth of our human condition — "... *for all have sinned and fall short of the glory of God...*" (Rom. 3:23). The Christian belief in original sin and depravity has always been alien and even offensive to many Cultural Chinese but they can certainly identify with sin in reality — in their own lives as much as in the lives of others.

Both Confucianism and the biblical worldview agree that most of us know what the basic moral principles are as guided by our conscience. There is a general consensus about what is good and what is evil and the common desire to pursue and do that which is good. Yet we find ourselves unable to put those moral principles fully into practice. Paul, in writing to the church in Rome, rightly points out the human dilemma — that we know what is right, but we lack the capacity to accomplish the right thing.[7] We possess moral knowledge but lack the ability to live it out — hence the old adage, "*Do as I say, not as I do.*" While the biblical faith recognizes this as the result of the sinful condition of humanity, the Confucian theory of the goodness of human nature attributes this failure to the evil or pervasive environment and ignorance.

However, this diagnosis falls short of giving an account of the source of evil. Hence it also fails to explain why benevolent and good people suffer. It merely draws our attention to the question of how the problem of evil can be solved by human beings.[8] Confucius himself was far from feeling assured of his own perfection. He was trying to build an ideology that can serve as a foundation upon which to pursue freedom, happiness and ultimately human flourishing. Unfortunately, he took the nature of man and society as he observed them as the basis of his ideology.[9] Hence, he said little about life after death and made little or no reference to it as a restraint to wickedness or a motivation to virtue.[10]

Since Confucianism believes the orientation towards good is inherent in everyone, it assumes that humanity in general has a common aspiration for self-cultivation. The success of Confucian ethics, therefore, presumes moral prescripts and actions as the autonomous realization of human nature that is inherently good. Any effort in moral self-cultivation is based on the autonomous will of an individual and not swayed by external imperatives or duty.[11]

In other words, we strive towards benevolence and other moral ideals because we instinctively want to. But this poses a dilemma when the circumstance is unfavorable to the practice of such moral ideals — as when there is no sufficient incentive for doing so. This is evident in the example cited of public apathy where there is not only no incentive to help the needy, but where kindness can be self-detrimental. This can result in indifference as well as a reduced sense of social responsibility and moral commitment.

In 2007, a student in China was ordered to pay more than $7,000 in compensation to an elderly woman whom he had taken to the hospital after a fall. She accused him of causing the accident. The court sided with the woman, believing that the student would not have bothered to help unless he was at fault.[12] Though new evidence seemed to indicate that he indeed was at fault, such incidents contribute to the growing apathy in China about helping strangers in need.

Though Confucius promoted the notion of the Mandate of Heaven, he is mostly silent concerning the existence of a personal God. Since Confucian ethics are commonly believed to be based on the goodness of human nature rather than on the divine personal being, the tension between ethical demand/duty and human limitation/weakness is often overlooked. However, our *a priori* assumptions about human nature, as well as where we ground morality, are crucial if we are to succeed in our self-cultivation.

James Legge rightly points out that Mencius's doctrine of human nature was defective because his ideal did not cover the whole field of duty — that there is no explicit affirmation of the divine implies that a person's moral duty or obligation is only unto himself or herself and the society; and will have no eternal significance.[13] When our moral obligation is perceived this way, even though autonomous, it will never bring us any closer to the Confucian ideals because unless there is divine intervention, our sinful condition will always taint our good intentions, no matter how noble.[14] In other words, Confucius suggests that we can actualize our full humanity by self-cultivation because we are inherently good. However, this is like pulling yourself up by your own bootstrap, and will remain an impossible task unless you are offered a helping hand.

On the other hand, the biblical faith recognizes that sin has corrupted humanity and contends that any form of self-cultivation must begin with solving the problem of sin and halting its pervasiveness. For that we will need divine intervention. And we know that that has come in the person of Christ. So, Pastor An is right — the ideals of the Noble Man and human flourishing are possible only when Cultural Chinese embrace the good news of Jesus Christ.

However, for the Christian faith to be considered and embraced without reservation by the Cultural Chinese as one that is relevant and not just another Western import, the historical baggage of Christianity will have to be overcome. And just as in all cross-cultural settings, one of the ways we can cultivate an open mind so that our unbelieving friends can be persuaded is to start from common ground rather than from where we differ.

In view of the historical disrepute that the Christian faith bears among the Cultural Chinese, we need to examine how we can present the gospel in a way that resonates with their aspirations and values — especially with regards to human flourishing as defined by the ideals of Confucianism. However, in trying to communicate a gospel that is culturally meaningful to the Cultural Chinese, it is useful to heed missiologist Paul Hiebert's counsel on contextualization:

> The foreignness of the culture we add to the gospel offends and must be eliminated. But the gospel itself offends. It is supposed to offend, and we dare not weaken its offense. The gospel must be contextualized, but it must remain prophetic. It must stand in judgment of what is evil in all cultures as well as in all persons.[15]

The Cultural Chinese Soul: an Obstacle or an Advantage?
Many resources on contextualization of the gospel have been written and it is common to find how the characteristics of the Cultural Chinese are deemed as barriers to their understanding and acceptance of the gospel. But this does not need to be the case. These traits or values of the Cultural Chinese may actually be an aid rather than a hindrance. Let us look at some of these characteristics and examine how the gospel would be meaningful against each of the traits or values discussed.

Many words can be used to describe the Cultural Chinese soul. In writing about China alone, Yu Hua used ten and aptly named his book *China in Ten Words*. Another writer used 57 in his book about the Chinese mind.[16] I would imagine that more adjectives are necessary if we include Diaspora Chinese as well. However, I shall limit myself simply to three:

1. **Harmonious relationships**

   For as long as the Chinese civilization is known to have existed, the great concern for Cultural Chinese has been with human relations.[17] This is evident even in their relationship with nature — instead of overcoming nature, Daoism promotes living harmoniously with it. It is believed that all of reality is interconnected — the harmonious working together of the forces in Heaven and Earth influences every individual and every event.[18]

   Between the Chinese philosophies of Daoism and Confucianism, the goals of achieving harmony, inner peace, learning to be fully human, moral cultivation and so on, are all closely related because they bring us closer to our "sagehood".[19] Though these two schools of philosophy have often been viewed as being in opposition, they differ only in emphases and ways to achieve the goals: Daoism seeks to establish harmonious rapport with nature while Confucianism seeks to preserve communal harmony within the social system. Together they address the question of how we can we live in harmony with ourselves, with nature and with others.[20]

   Hence it is not surprising that this principle of harmony governs the social life of the Cultural Chinese as well. It is widely known that the Chinese culture is a face-value culture that greatly honors relationships (*guanxi*). While the notion of *guanxi* is too complex to discuss here, suffice it to say that Cultural Chinese would try to avoid confrontation at all times and at all costs to maintain the harmony of their relationships.

   In all aspects of life — family, business and friendships — nobody should cause someone to lose face and run the risk of severing the relationship. The significance of maintaining the harmony of familial relationships is especially evident during festive seasons when members of the extended family come together for the celebratory dinner (often a banquet of at least eight courses!).

Any Cultural Chinese would recognize the significance of the Chinese New Year's eve reunion dinner as an opportune time to make good any misunderstandings that exist between members of the family. The rule is, regardless how badly someone in the family has wronged you, or no matter how annoying Uncle Chen is, you are to be nice and to treat him respectfully — especially if he is older than you. In other words, even when you are in the right, you should avoid any conflict to make things right. Truth is irrelevant because maintaining harmony is sacrosanct.

I remember as a teenager, I would loathe having to make nice with a certain relative, Uncle Tan, who always annoyed me with his snarky remarks. As far as I was concerned, he was judgmental and calculative! Nonetheless, I had to be respectful because, "No matter what, he is family!" my mother would remind me, despite my protests that he did not deserve to be my uncle. *"There shouldn't be any overnight vengeance,"* as the Cantonese saying goes. I have never understood why this was so important to my parents until I got married. Having married into a different culture gave me the advantage of being able to dissect and understand my Chinese culture in comparison to another.

For example, if my husband did not like his uncle, John, his mother would never insist that he ought to be nice to John at Christmas dinners — especially when he's an adult. In fact, if he wanted, my husband could opt out of the dinner if John was going to be there! However, such a gesture (especially towards a relative who is older) would be considered extremely rude and would never be tolerated in my family or in most Chinese families. Similarly, if you saw Uncle Tan on a date with a woman other than his wife, you would be discouraged from calling him out on his adultery because that would cause him to lose face as well as disrupt the harmony of relationships — between you and him as well as between him and his wife.

Our relationships with those whom we share blood relations will always have precedence over other relationships. When I was a college sophomore, I had to take a class in photography. Since we could not afford a camera then, I decided to borrow one from my uncle — my father's younger brother. After all that my father had done to help him find a job and take him into our home when he was jobless, I thought that the loan would be a given. To my great disappointment (and resentment for many years!), he refused to let me use his camera for a few months. I complained endlessly to my mother about how ungrateful my uncle was and how I would have nothing to do with him henceforth. My mother's response to my legitimate grievances was that I should forgive him and let the matter go because, after all, he is a (blood) relation. Cultural Chinese are commonly expected to forgive those in the family unconditionally — just because they are related by blood.

While avoiding open conflict and preserving the harmony of relationships often take precedence over doing what is morally right and true, it does not mean that Cultural Chinese do not value their morality. In fact, it is likely that morally wrong behavior is deemed shameful and would bring disrepute but no one wants to risk the harmony of his or her relationships to deal with it.

However, our biblical faith informs us that sin will always disrupt the harmony of our relationships no matter how hard we attempt to preserve them because the peace of our ultimate relationship with God has been damaged. It will not be difficult for Cultural Chinese to see how and why our severed ties with our Heavenly Father affects all our relationships, because they understand very well the importance of their filial bonds. Within the context of a Cultural Chinese family, sin is perceived as an act that brings dishonor to the family's reputation as well as shame to the community of which the wrong-doer is a part. The shame and dishonor in turn disrupt the harmony of the community.[21]

Modern Western discussions of sin and atonement have tended to raise the question of guilt, but sin within the biblical narrative clearly incorporates the aspect of shame, too. This is why the story of the prodigal son in the New Testament is a persuasive narrative for a Cultural Chinese because it deals with elements of honor, shame, filial piety and restoration of relationships.

Hence, the Good News is significant to the Cultural Chinese because it restores the relationship of humanity with the Heavenly Father, which, in turn, positively affects all our relationships. The harmony the gospel is able to bring to our relationships — with the Heavenly Father, with oneself (self-acceptance, identity), and with others — cannot be overstated and is especially meaningful for a people who are so concerned with maintaining harmony in all of life.

2. **Ethnocentric**

While the term ethnocentric may typically have a negative connotation, this term is used somewhat neutrally here. A Cultural Chinese is unapologetically proud of his or her ethnic heritage and culture (and cuisine). Though a third-generation Chinese in Malaysia, I will never pass on any opportunity to educate my half-Caucasian son on the achievements of the ancient Chinese civilizations. Once, in frustration, he retorted, "So what if the Chinese invented all these things, Americans invented superheroes!"

Cultural Chinese's ethnocentrism is first evident in the way ancient Chinese refer to themselves — the proper name of China in Mandarin literally means Middle or Central Kingdom. This name was adopted in medieval times when the Chinese considered themselves the most advanced people in the known ancient world and believed that they were the center of the world. People of neighboring nations and elsewhere were considered barbarians.[22] China's thousands of years of history have given the Chinese a sense of superiority about their culture.

This strong sense of ethnic identity and pride has been a great resistance to the infiltration of the gospel. Her isolation from other early civilizations also led the Chinese to believe that they were the most cultured, the most intelligent and the most capable of men. This belief was of course not challenged until the middle of the nineteenth century, when China was defeated in war and her sovereignty was wrestled away by a series of political treaties.[23]

In describing Cultural Chinese around the world, H.G. Creel remarked that the Chinese "have always had, for as long as the record runs, a fierce and unquenchable national pride exceeded by that of no other people. In Paris or San Francisco or Singapore, Chinese are still Chinese even after generations of sojourn. They seem all but unalterable."[24]

Our ethnocentrism comes also in part from our belief that we are a self-sufficient people. In 1793, British Lord Macartney was sent on a diplomatic mission to the court of the Qianlong emperor to expand trade with China. However, he was unsuccessful in his venture and his failure has become a classic statement of how China viewed herself in relation to the rest of the world. The Chinese emperor refused to listen to British demands and ordered Macartney to perform the *kowtow* and sent the following reply to the British king regarding the expansion of trade:

> Our Celestial Empire possesses all things in prolific abundance, and lacks no products within its borders. I set no value on objects strange or ingenious, and have no use for your country's manufactures. There is therefore no need to import the manufactures of your country in exchange for our own products.[25]

The message closed with words that betrayed how the Chinese emperor perceived China's relationship with the rest of the world:

> It behoves you, O King, to respect my sentiments, and to display even greater devotion and loyalty in future, so that by perpetual submission to our Throne, you may secure peace and prosperity for your country thereafter.[26]

While these words may seem absurd, missiologist George Hood claims that "no one understands China until this document has ceased to seem absurd." He adds that one will never fully understand the Chinese if one judges China by Western criteria and assumptions that have been imposed or willingly adopted in other parts of the world.

If China was self-sufficient materially, it believed it more so in the realm of social ethics, philosophy and religion.[27] In fact, it is this sense of self-sufficiency that has contributed to China's hostility to the modern missionary movement — why the need for a foreign, especially Western religion or God when we already have a pantheon of them (gods and sages) and philosophies that are older that Christianity? However, as discussed, Confucianism which is most dominant in the worldview of a Cultural Chinese, has fallen short as the path to their existential aspirations.

Today, Cultural Chinese are known everywhere for their resourcefulness and work ethic. In their understated ways, they strive with discipline and determination against all odds to achieve their goals. It is this "Can Do" approach to life that has brought success and a better life to millions of diaspora Chinese around the world. Similarly, the Cultural Chinese's resourcefulness has contributed much to the economic success of China, resulting in it being one of the largest economies of today. The same can be said of countries where the majority of their populations are Cultural Chinese, like Singapore, Hong Kong and Taiwan.

In describing the drivenness of the Chinese, journalist Boye Lafayatte De Menthe writes of the vast number of ordinary people in China today that are so driven by the desire to succeed financially that they work in a kind of frenzy. Many are so caught up in the challenges and opportunities that they disregard any moral or ethical concerns in their pursuits.[28]

This is the flipside to the self-sufficiency — a fearless resourcefulness that led my late maternal grandfather to a life of piracy: *GungGung* apparently was a master counterfeiter. For example, he analyzed the chemical content of Guinness Stout and figured out how to make bootleg stout! Apparently it tasted just like the real thing and was, in fact, stout except that it forged the Guinness trademark. The law caught up with him but he managed to gull one of his mistresses to take the fall. This did not stop him from counterfeiting again — this time he concocted chicken essence and sold it under a popular trademark.[29] I heard that he made a small fortune through his various counterfeiting businesses — an educated man who obviously had a penchant for chemistry and achieved reasonable financial success, but he was morally corrupt.

Both the ethnocentrism and self-sufficiency of the Cultural Chinese may lead them to dismiss the gospel which is perceived as foreign or even Western. However, if we can find a way to locate biblical truths within the Cultural Chinese's culture, then we would be able to convince them that the Christian God is not foreign and has also revealed himself and certain truths to the Chinese — as is the case.

3. Pragmatic and utilitarian

Philosopher Winfried Corduan, in evaluating the effectiveness of conventional Christian apologetics to the Cultural Chinese quips, "As I've heard it expressed numerous times, the fundamental Chinese attitude seems to be that if something is supposed to be a deity, you might as well worship it. If it turns out that it is a god, you did well. If it was not really a god, you just wasted a few seconds of your time."[30]

I can certainly identify with this form of pragmatism because it was my then non-believing mother's pragmatism which insisted that I go to Sunday School (to learn good behavior). But God used the opportunity to plant the seed of the gospel in my life. Similarly, it was my maternal grandmother's (*PohPoh's*) pragmatic approach to religion that led my mother to encounter Jesus. As *PohPoh* wanted to ensure that her only son, a Christian, would attend her funeral when she died, she decided to go to church and be a Christian like him. As she did not want to attend church on her own, my mother, the filial daughter that she is, started accompanying *PohPoh* to Sunday service.

Soon God was working in my mother's heart and she began to feel conflicted — she was starting to believe what she heard preached about Jesus but she would go home to a house with an altar laden with traditional Chinese gods. However, she told no one and kept this dilemma in her heart. One day, a lady at church approached her and asked if she was conflicted. My mother was surprised as she had told no one. The lady went on to challenge her — if she wanted to know whether Jesus was the true God, she should pray to him for three things that meant a lot to her. So my mother did. And within a month, God answered her prayers — all three things that she had prayed for came through. A week later all the Chinese gods and statuettes in her house were removed and she accepted Jesus as her Lord and Savior. While I am not advocating that we "test" Jesus like my mother did, God in his loving grace revealed himself to her in a way that she knew.

It is common to find Cultural Chinese adhering to a religion for the benefits that it will reap for them. Often religious practices are observed out of an immediate and practical need — such as healing from sickness, protection from harm, or career success. This means belief and subscription to a religion or faith is based on its efficacy rather than on whether it is true or not. The pragmatic Cultural Chinese would accept gods and beliefs as necessary — even when they are contradictory. This is a somewhat pluralist approach to faith or religion, where faith is perceived as a means to attain utilitarian benefits and, hence, the more gods and spirits one believes in, the better it will be.[31]

Traditional Chinese religions have a very strong utilitarian feature because this characteristic of the Cultural Chinese has definitely influenced the evolution of Daoism, Confucianism and Buddhism. As these three schools of thought are wide open systems (as opposed to canonical and creedal belief systems like Islam or Christianity), their ideological adaptation to the pragmatism and utilitarianism of the Cultural Chinese is evident in the various forms in which they exist today to satisfy the psychological needs of the adherent: Daoism's pantheon of gods serve the various wishes of the worshipper while Buddhism helps to release souls from the 18-level purgatory.[32] This is why arguing about the truth of these belief systems in evangelistic apologetics often fail because it is difficult to expose the inconsistency of a worldview where the constituting systems of beliefs are not fundamentally defined and are based on the subjective experience of the adherent.

Unfortunately, the Christianity that many of us are familiar with today, due to influence of the Enlightenment, is one that dichotomizes the world into the spiritual and physical, the unseen and seen, religion and science, subjective values and objective facts, and the sacred and secular. On the other hand, much of Asia does not perceive of life in such a dichotomized way. Human life is holistic and communal.[33] Hence, Christianity may be seen as incompatible with the Cultural Chinese's understanding of life.

However, this is a false contradiction because as we have discussed in a previous chapter, true biblical faith corresponds with our experience of reality as spiritual and physical and it is livable in practical terms. The Christian faith ought to be understood, lived and witnessed as such — a grand narrative, a worldview that is holistic and encompasses all of life — seen and unseen. Hence, *true biblical faith* which concerns not just life beyond death but also our immediate life on earth would resonate meaningfully within the Cultural Chinese's pragmatic outlook on life. A note of caution though — because of their pragmatic attitude towards faith, they are also fertile harvesting grounds for false beliefs like the prosperity gospel or the Hyper Grace teachings.

In addition, the individualism we see in present-day Christianity is not part of the biblical heritage but rather a cultural shift from the emphasis on community to individual. As a result, the Christian faith is commonly perceived as one that is exceedingly individualistic, such that when one becomes a follower of Jesus, one would cease to be interested in matters concerning the family. Hence if we are to portray the attractiveness of the gospel, there is a great need for us to also look to stories in the Old Testament, such as Ruth, that exemplify the kinsman-redeemer ideal where we readily come to the aid of our relatives — the neglected, the sick and infirm, and the forgotten elderly.[34]

On a lighter note about pragmatism, a Chinese Christian once wrote that since the worship of the Christ does not require the use of joss sticks and other forms of material offerings, it is a more economical religion to follow. Apparently, a folk rhyme even exists to summarize this notion:

> *It is really worthwhile to believe in Jesus, one neither drinks (alcohol) nor smokes, one does not have to burn joss sticks and paper-money, and one will not gamble either; in such a way one can save much money every year. When money is saved, one*

may have a better life, and after death one can go into heaven.
Please tell me, whether this is worthwhile or not?[35]

God's General Revelation: Confucius Paved the Way

Cultural Chinese are pragmatic in their outlook, ethnocentric in
their identity and greatly value harmony especially in their social
relationships. Is it possible to present the gospel of Jesus Christ to
Cultural Chinese effectively against these three characteristics? Beyond
seeking for points of relevance, it is remarkable that God has shown his
mercy and grace through general revelation of truth to all peoples and
nations:

> *For the wrath of God is revealed from heaven against all ungodliness*
> *and unrighteousness of men, who by their unrighteousness suppress*
> *the truth. For what can be known about God is plain to them, because*
> *God has shown it to them. For his invisible attributes, namely, his*
> *eternal power and divine nature, have been clearly perceived, ever*
> *since the creation of the world, in the things that have been made. So*
> *they are without excuse.* (Rom. 1:18–20)

General revelation refers to the knowledge of God's existence as well
as the knowledge of right and wrong that can be discerned in our
experience of the world. This general revelation of God is known by
everyone.[36] In addition, there is a natural order of morality written on
the hearts of all people:

> *For when Gentiles, who do not have the law, by nature do what the*
> *law requires, they are a law to themselves, even though they do not*
> *have the law. They show that the work of the law is written on their*
> *hearts, while their conscience also bears witness, and their conflicting*
> *thoughts accuse or even excuse them on that day when, according*
> *to my gospel, God judges the secrets of men by Christ Jesus.* (Rom.
> 2:14–16)

However, this knowledge of right and wrong can be suppressed or
obscured by many factors as a consequence of sin. For instance,
traditional practices or values may hamper our access to truth but
our culture could also provide the context in which we may encounter
the one true God. Culture is the means and never the ultimate goal
because when we make any cultural ideal, preference, or aspiration so
central, we place it in competition with God who is the only ultimate.

So the question for us is whether the Chinese culture provides the context for Cultural Chinese to encounter God and His salvation. Based on the nature of God and his Word, the answer would be a resounding yes:

> [W]e bring you good news, that you should turn from these vain things to a living God, who made the heaven and the earth and the sea and all that is in them. In past generations he allowed all the nations to walk in their own ways. Yet he did not leave himself without witness, for he did good by giving you rains from heaven and fruitful seasons, satisfying your hearts with food and gladness. (Acts 14:15–17)

There is a common existential recognition that is found across civilizations and cultures — that something has gone awry with humanity, impeding our ability to fulfill our destiny. Hence there is a need to find the way to resolve this existential crisis of humanity.

In Confucius's terms, he concluded that the sociopolitical chaos of his days were a result of the abuse of *li* (ritual/propriety) by the rulers. Instead of fulfilling their heavenly mandated duties (as custodians of their citizens), they were more preoccupied with their self-interests and employed immoral ways to achieve them. Under the charge of such corrupt men, the common man suffered — individually and as a society.

If virtues were taught and lived then humanity can be restored and would make progress towards their destiny of becoming the Noble Man. When we get these fundamental principles right we will experience harmony in our social relationships, between individuals and within families, while the state will experience peace and prosperity. Such a utopian society will in turn serve as a conducive environment for self-cultivation and human flourishing.

In the previous chapter, we highlighted aspects of both Confucius's ideal of a utopian society and the shalomic vision of the biblical faith. What may be apparent are the various aspects that are similar between them. First of all, both are concerned with humanity's existential crisis and see human flourishing as part of our destiny. They also believe moral transformation and harmonious relationships are crucial towards the realization of our humanity — it is what it means to be human. These parallels seem to indicate that Confucius was familiar with the truth that Yahweh has mercifully revealed to all peoples.

Central to the shalomic vision in the Christian Scripture is that all of creation can exist harmoniously in community with each other, thriving and pursuing the joy and well-being of every other creature because it is built on and centers on the will of its God (Isa. 2:2–4).[37] In the Old Testament, this shalomic reality is described as a single family, members of a single tribe, heirs of a single hope, and bearers of a single destiny when Abraham is affirmed as the father of all Israel and every person is his child (Gen. 15:5; Isa. 41:8, 51:2). In the New Testament, the Church has a parallel vision of all peoples being invited to the lordship and fellowship of Jesus (Matt. 28:16–20; John 12:32) and eventually into a single shalomic community:[38]

> *After this I looked, and behold, a great multitude that no one could number, from every nation, from all tribes and peoples and languages, standing before the throne and before the Lamb, clothed in white robes, with palm branches in their hands, and crying out with a loud voice, "Salvation belongs to our God who sits on the throne, and to the Lamb!"… "Therefore they are before the throne of God, and serve him day and night in his temple; and he who sits on the throne will shelter them with his presence. They shall hunger no more, neither thirst anymore; the sun shall not strike them, nor any scorching heat. For the Lamb in the midst of the throne will be their shepherd, and he will guide them to springs of living water, and God will wipe away every tear from their eyes.* (Rev. 7:9–10, 15–17)

The welfare of the shalomic community is not contingent upon the absence of threats. When life is anchored in obedience to Yahweh, *shalom* is present even in the midst of threats — from war, starvation or danger. In Leviticus 26, the vision is laid out for the faithful as well as the disobedient.

According to Brueggemann, the flourishing promised to those who are obedient is grounded in reality and history, and not the idyllic "pie in the sky" variety. It is well-being in the midst of threats and enemies — in the very situations where people always have to grapple with anxiety, poverty or temptation. While it is a flourishing of a very personal kind, it is also deliberately communal and not only for the insulated/reclusive individuals. It is flourishing for the whole community regardless of age, sex or socioeconomic status. In fact, this biblical *shalom* comes only to the inclusive, embracing community that excludes none.[39] Hence, in the shalomic vision, there is no place for oppression and division.

Similarly, Confucius saw that the pursuit of human flourishing is not a private project. It involves not just reclusive self-cultivated individuals but Noble Men and Women who live out their virtues and social obligations/duties in family and community. Similar to how biblical *shalom* is experienced, Noble Men and Women are not intimidated by the challenges of life because suffering and threats are perceived as means of self-cultivation. (Mencius 4B:15)

The ideal Confucian society is built on the foundation of harmonious relationships akin to a universal family (Analects 12:5). The principle that enables solidarity and peace in the ideal Confucian society includes the duty of practicing *ren* (benevolence or civility) in all of our relationships. If successful, this would also mean that oppression and corruption would cease, as those who govern would do so in kindness and justice.

Unfortunately, the success of the Confucian project seems to have been thwarted by the weakness of its very driving force — humanity itself. This is, of course, not unique to Confucianism. The other two religions of China, Daoism and Buddhism, equally promote the notion of self-redemption — that humans can be redeemed through their own efforts, that through their own efforts they can gain self-inner transcendence. In fact, the pursuit of all three traditions is embodied in some form of inner-transcendence: Confucianism (becoming the sage-like Noble Man), Buddhism (becoming a Buddha) and Daoism (becoming an immortal).[40]

However, one significant distinction is that Confucius taught that sagehood is to be sought within society while Buddhists and Daoists retreat from society to practice their spiritual disciplines in solitude. In other words, while Confucianism's other-dependent aspect distinguishes it from most Eastern religions, it is comparable to the need for external intervention (of God) in the biblical faith. Nonetheless, Confucianism's starting point in the quest of human flourishing lies in the will of individuals. But as we have noted, if humanity is its own measure of progress, then we will not get very far.

Fortunately, the shortcomings of humanity were not lost on Confucius and his followers. Mencius, despite his optimistic view that human nature is good, admitted that it does not imply that humans are always entirely good. Instead, he believed that men will surely make mistakes but it was in the continual correction of their shortcomings that human progress lay:[41]

> *Men for the most part err, and are afterwards able to reform. They are distressed in and and perplexed in their thoughts, and then they arise to vigorous reformation. When things have been evidenced in men's looks, and set forth in their words, then they understand them.* (Mencius 6B:15)[42]

Mencius, in his appraisal of human nature, drew conclusions that particularly shaped the Confucian view of the relationship between Heaven and humanity: he believed that if humans derived their good nature from Heaven, then Heaven must be good. And as the source of goodness, Heaven was the supreme judge and authority of human morality. Secondly, self-cultivation did not just develop a person's morality, it also accumulated righteousness for him or her because by self-cultivation, one was serving Heaven.[43]

Confucian scholar Yao XinZhong concluded that a crucial fundamental belief about the Heaven-human relationship resulted from this understanding: if Heaven was the source of moral goodness, then humanity's ultimate moral duty was to Heaven and not merely to himself, family or society.[44] Regrettably, we can only speculate what Confucius and his followers' believed about the nature of Heaven as the Confucian concerns were predominantly this-worldly.

However, what is insufficiently alluded to in Confucius's teachings about the divine is clearly revealed in the New Testament. In the first century AD, Paul found himself among Athenians whose view of the world and approach to religion was strikingly similar to the Cultural Chinese's, where idolatry was ubiquitous and many different types of religions and philosophies abounded. It was a context that was highly pluralistic with worldviews that were very diverse and distant from the Judeo-Christian tradition. In his sermon on Mars Hill, he proclaimed to the religious Athenians what had been specially revealed through the Christ:

> *What therefore you worship as unknown, this I proclaim to you. The God who made the world and everything in it, being Lord of heaven and earth, does not live in temples made by man, nor is he served by human hands, as though he needed anything, since he himself gives to all mankind life and breath and everything. And he made*

from one man every nation of mankind to live on all the face of the earth, having determined allotted periods and the boundaries of their dwelling place, that they should seek God, and perhaps feel their way toward him and find him. Yet he is actually not far from each one of us, for "'In him we live and move and have our being'..." (Acts 17:23b–28a)

Here we see Paul appealing to the universality of the Christian message that, fundamentally, the Christian faith was grounded in the fact that the Creator of the heavens and earth had revealed truth about himself and humanity. This truth that is centered in the person and work of Jesus Christ needs to be both believed and acted upon if humanity is to be restored (to a proper relationship with God).

God's Special Revelation: Jesus is the Way

So far we have seen a strong parallel in the many aspects of Confucius's ideal of human flourishing and the biblical vision of *shalom* in addressing the inadequacy of the human condition. However, what has fallen short in Confucius's solution was his optimism in the very nature of humanity that needs restoration. He maintained that humanity's flaws were the fruits of a bad or evil environment but he never went on to account for how our environment turned bad/evil — the root of evil which is sin. When we take a realistic and honest consideration of human nature, we know that we will never be able to achieve human flourishing on our own merit and ability. Hence, Confucius's insight of the plight of humanity is accurate and serves to pave the way for the special revelation of the Son of God in the person of Christ.

If the root cause of the human dilemma lies within humanity itself, then we will need external non-human intervention to help us root out the source of our plight. And this is where the Good News for the Cultural Chinese comes in. The aspiration of human flourishing and becoming a Noble Man may be unattainable on our own, but we do not have to do it on our own. The path towards that hope is open to us in Christ:

For I bear them witness that they have a zeal for God, but not according to knowledge. For, being ignorant of the righteousness of God, and seeking to establish their own, they did not submit to God's righteousness. For Christ is the end of the law for righteousness to everyone who believes. (Rom. 10:2–4)

Jesus said to him, "I am the way, and the truth, and the life. No one comes to the Father except through me." (John 14:6)

Much of what is central to the Cultural Chinese's attainment of human flourishing is the quality of one's relationships. Maintaining the goodwill of existing relationships towards a harmonious society and an inner harmony is all part of Confucius's notion of human flourishing. But it is evident that we will not achieve true peace in our relationships as long as we are broken and affected by sin. And the only way for us to be restored from the brokenness and consequence of sin is to first mend our relationship with God. In other words, for us to find harmony in our social relationships, we must first seek to be reconciled to the Heavenly Father.

However, the Heavenly Father is sovereign and already has a plan to save us. Just like the Cultural Chinese, God values harmony and unity.[45] He opposes estrangement and disintegration. He longs to see the damages of sin eliminated. He wants his creation to be reconciled to himself because that is the way it ought to be. Humanity and all of creation will not find its ultimate purpose unless they are in a harmonious and loving relationship with God.

The one sent to reverse the effects of sin has been announced — God the Father sends his Son, the perfect servant, to initiate His vision of Shalom. In Isaiah 40, the prophecy of this perfect Servant describes him as one who fills God with delight, he is quiet and gentle, faithful and persevering; he does not falter or become discouraged, and so on. Now that we have the advantage of perspective, we see that the servant referred to in this passage was not an ideal for Israel to aspire to (like Confucius's Noble Man) but a real person who is God's answer to humanity's weakness and failure.[46]

It is through Jesus, the Son of God that God's purposes for his creation will be realized — the shalomic vision begins to unfold as a reality. He has come to reverse all the destructive effects sin has had on humanity and to restore to people their true purpose and freedom as sons and daughters of God. The work of the servant ushered in the prospect of God's glory being displayed in His relationship with his people and with the world.[47]

Though the Mandate of Heaven was a term commonly used to refer to one's fate in the Cultural Chinese context, Confucius used it to speak of the will of God. He believed the emperor held the key to the Mandate of Heaven and hence was deemed to be the Son of Heaven. As he is the Son of Heaven and appointed to reign, he is the mediator between the powers above and the people below, governing by the Mandate of Heaven.[48] Unfortunately, China's ancient past informs us that most of the earthly Sons of Heaven proved to have failed in their mission to govern wisely. Over time, the temptation of great power corrupted the throne. Hence *Shangdi*,[49] in His grace and mercy, decided to send His own — the true Son of Heaven:

> *Behold, the days are coming, declares the LORD, when I will raise up for David a righteous Branch, and he shall reign as king and deal wisely, and shall execute justice and righteousness in the land.* (Jer. 23:5)

Unlike his predecessors, this Son of Heaven came to rule and to serve, and to fulfill the will of *Shangdi*. Since he came from *Shangdi* Himself, he was not corrupted by sin like other sons of Heaven. Through his life, King Jesus sets an example of how humanity ought to live. Jesus understood filial piety as it led him to sacrifice his life to fulfill the mission the Father gave him. In order for him to restore harmony to all creation, he had to first reconcile all men to *Shangdi*.

He did this by fulfilling the obligation that humanity owed *Shangdi* — that is, death.

Humanity is sentenced to death because we have rejected the lordship of God, dishonoring Him and causing him shame. However, Jesus, out of his obedience and love for his Father, was willing to take that punishment on our behalf. He died for all men (and women) and whoever accepts that truth and is willing to grant lordship of their life over to Jesus, He also sends the Holy Spirit to help him or her live righteously and virtuously.

With our relationship to the Heavenly Father restored through the work of the Son of Heaven, and the help of the Holy Spirit in our self-cultivation, humanity will begin to experience the human flourishing that the shalomic vision describes. When the narrative of the gospel is presented this way, Cultural Chinese will find it more comprehensible and familiar because it corresponds with Confucius's ideals for humanity, but with a realistic solution. It also mitigates the risk of being considered a Western religion.

My mother became a follower of Jesus after having been a worshipper of traditional Chinese gods for almost 40 years. I once asked her what is the one thing she loves most about her life in Christ and she replied that it was her personal relationship with God: "I can now pray to Shangdi and know that he has heard me and will answer my prayers because he is a loving Father."

Scripture also tells us that Jesus is the one mediator between man and God: *"For there is one God, and there is one mediator between God and men, the man Christ Jesus, who gave himself as a ransom for all, which is the testimony given at the proper time."* (1 Tim. 2:5–6) That the Chinese culture is a face-value culture that greatly honors relationships (*guanxi*) means confrontation is never done directly but via an emissary or mediator to mitigate the risk of loss of face. Match-made marriages and the engaging of a reputable person as guarantor rather than signing a contract are all cultural practices that are familiar to the Cultural Chinese.

Since Cultural Chinese are very well acquainted with the need for and the role of a mediator or middle person in any major undertaking, we can certainly present Jesus as the mediator, and reconciler of relationships — Jesus restores humanity's vertical relationship with God as well as the horizontal relationship with one's fellow man.[50]

In addition, within the Chinese shame-honor culture, what Jesus did on the Cross becomes very powerful for the Cultural Chinese when it is seen as "Christ's shame-bearing death." And as we demonstrate how the resurrection is "honor-gaining", the gospel narrative immediately becomes recognizable and indeed very desirable.[51]

Conclusion

This discussion was born out of a personal frustration at being called a traitor to the Chinese culture because I follow a supposedly Western God. This posed a problem for me because it is my desire to see many Cultural Chinese come to experience the truth and hope that is found only in Christ. That the gospel of Jesus Christ needs to be shared relevantly to Cultural Chinese led me to examine the teachings of Laozi, Confucius and Siddharta Gautama against the biblical worldview.

What I discovered was how similar Confucius's ideal self and society were to the biblical vision of *shalom*. It soon became apparent to me that Paul was right — God has indeed left us imprints of himself and his truth (Rom. 1:18–20) so that we would seek him and find him (Acts 17:26, 27). God in his richness has created cultural diversity within the human race. Unfortunately, just as sin has tainted everything else in creation, human cultures, too, have been ruined by the influence of sinful values. However, God is continually pursuing his people in their varied cultural settings so that they may turn to and serve him. His daily providence and blessings testify to his care and concern for all people. He did not leave any generation without witness to him and we are all responsible for the truth which we have received because he does not hold us responsible for what we have not been taught but for the teaching we choose to ignore (Rom. 2:14–15).

While God has chosen to accomplish his plan of salvation and his shalomic vision within the Jewish culture and context, the truth that is the person of Christ is for all humankind, irrespective of ethnicity, culture, or religion, because all are sinners and in need of redemption by God's grace. If we are to be faithful to the task that Christ assigned us — in making disciples of all nations (Matt. 28: 19, 20), then we must also be diligent in learning about the cultural roadblocks that are standing in the way of the nations embracing the Christian faith as their own, and seek to articulate the gospel in terms that are attractive and significant to the peoples of the nations.

In the case of the Cultural Chinese, I concur with Sinologist Paulos Huang: "Thus, Christian missionary work is, in fact, to help the Chinese people rediscover their own God whom they have forgotten."[52]

Let us make it so.

ENDNOTES

Chapter 1

[1] Cultural Chinese funeral rites are elaborate as they are believed to determine the destiny of the deceased in the Netherworld. The one who holds the key to the deceased's destiny is the deceased's male offspring. This will be further discussed in subsequent chapters.

[2] "Cultural Chinese" is a term derived from "Global China," one coined by modern Confucianist, Tu WeiMing, to describe the various Chinese societies. These include Chinese nationals as well as diaspora Chinese that are scattered globally. Another term that is commonly used to refer to these Chinese is "Global China".

[3] In the Mandarin Bible, the Greek term "Logos" in John's Gospel is translated as "Dao".

[4] Zhi Yong, "Is Christianity Contrary to Chinese Traditional Culture," March 5, 2017, http://chinachristiandaily.com/2017-03-05/culture/is-christianity-contrary-to-chinese-traditional-culture-_4262.html, accessed March 14, 2017.

[5] Choong Chee Pang, "A Response to Professor Wang Xiaochao's Five Misunderstandings about Christianity in Chinese Academic Circles," in *Christianity and Chinese Culture*, ed. Miikka Ruokanen and Paulos Huang Zhanzhu (Grand Rapids, MI: Eerdmans, 2000), 254.

[6] "Cultural Chinese" is used in certain contexts (as opposed to Chinese) as it is a broader term to include all diaspora Chinese from around the world — Singapore, Thailand, Vietnam, the Philippines, etc; as well as those from Mainland China.

[7] Wu Xiaoxin, "The Hall of Four: politics, faith and daily life in a northern Chinese village," April 16, 2010, accessed 21 July, 2013, http://podcasts.ox.ac.uk/people/xiaoxin-wu.

[8] This era of the Opium Wars and Unequal Treaties is also sometimes known as China's Century of Humiliation. And rightly so!

[9] George A. Hood, *Neither Bang nor Whimper* (Singapore: Presbyterian Church, 1991), 3.

[10] Jiang Menglin as quoted by Chen YongTao. "The Sinicization of Christianity: A Chinese Christian's Thoughts." *Chinese Theological Review*, 27 (2015): 125.

[11] He GuangHu, "The Compatibility of Christianity with the Traditional Chinese Religions in Their Theories of the Divinity," in *Christianity and Chinese Culture*, ed., Ruokanen and Paulos Huang Zhanzhu (Grand Rapids, MI: Eerdmans, 2000), 73.

[12] Hood, 6.

[13] *Nanking Massacre*, https://youtu.be/ILS6wGvOWO8 is a powerful and moving historical documentary based on Iris Chang's *The Rape of Nanking*. It documents the Westerners who decided to stay in Nanking to help the locals as the Japanese military pounded the city to dust.

[14] Tu WeiMing, "Quest for Meaning," in *Desecularization of the world: resurgent religion and world politics*, ed., Peter L Berger (Washington, DC: Ethics and Public Policy Center; Grand Rapids, MI: Eerdmans, 1999), 92.

[15] Zhuo XinPing, "Comprehensive Theology: An Attempt to Combine Christianity with Chinese Culture," in *Christianity and Chinese Culture*, ed., Ruokanen and Paulos Huang Zhanzhu (Grand Rapids, MI: Eerdmans, 2000), 189.

[16] Winfried Corduan, "More on Chinese Popular Religions and Apologetics," August 24, 2010, accessed 9 February, 2015, http://wincorduan.bravejournal.com/entry/54392/.

[17] Udo Middelmann, *Christianity versus Fatalistic Religions in the War against Poverty* (Colorado Springs, CO: Paternoster, 2007), 97–99.

[18] Corduan, "More on Chinese Popular Religions and Apologetics."

Chapter 2

1. A.W. Tozer, *I Call It Heresy* (Harrisburg, PA: Christian Publications, 1974), 5.
2. Harold Netland and Keith Yandell, *Buddhism: A Christian exploration and appraisal* (Downers Grove, IL: InterVarsity Press, 2009), 197.
3. Lesslie Newbigin, *Gospel in a Pluralist Society* (Grand Rapids, MI: Eerdmans, 1989), 13.
4. Charles Colson and Nancey Pearcey, *How Now Shall We Live?* (Carol Stream, IL: Tyndale House, 1999), 14.
5. Colson and Pearcey, 15.
6. Colson and Pearcey, 14.
7. John H. Kok, "Learning to Teach from Within a Christian Perspective," *Pro Rege* 31.4 (2003): 11–19.
8. Udo Middelmann, *Christianity versus Fatalistic Religions in the War against Poverty* (Colorado Springs, CO: Paternoster, 2008), 8.
9. Middelmann,17–33.
10. Middelmann, 20.
11. Middelmann, 21.
12. Middelmann, 25.
13. Middelmann, 10.
14. Colson and Pearcey, 14.
15. G.K. Chesterton, *Heretics* (North Yorkshire, UK: House of Stratus, 2001), 3.
16. Kevin J. Vanhoozer, "What is Everyday Theology? How and Why Christians Should Read Culture," in *Everyday Theology: How to read cultural texts and interpret trends*, ed., Kevin J. Vanhoozer, Charles A. Anderson and Michael J. Sleasman (Grand Rapids, MI: Baker Academic, 2007), 31.
17. Vanhoozer, "What is Everyday Theology," 32.
18. Vanhoozer, "What is Everyday Theology," 31.
19. Colson and Pearcey, 13.
20. Jackson Wu, *Saving God's Face: A Chinese contextualization of salvation through honor and shame* (Pasadena, CA: WCIU Press, 2012), 44–45.
21. Vanhoozer, "What is Everyday Theology," 7.
22. Vanhoozer, "What is Everyday Theology," 19.
23. Wu, 48.
24. Harold Netland, *Encountering Religious Pluralism: The challenge to Christian faith and mission* (Downers Grove, IL: InterVarsity Press, 2001), 247–8.
25. Netland, 13.
26. G.K. Chesterton, *The Everlasting Man* (San Francisco, CA: Ignatius Press, 1993), 213.
27. James W. Sire, *Why Good Arguments Fail: Making a more persuasive case for Christ* (Downers Grove, IL: InterVarsity Press, 2006), 140.
28. See Don Richardson, *Peace Child* (Ventura, CA: Regal, 1974).

Chapter 3

1. Tu WeiMing, "Quest for Meaning," in *Desecularization of the world: resurgent religion and world politics*, ed., Peter L. Berger (Washington, DC: Ethics and Public Policy Center; Grand Rapids, MI: Eerdmans, 1999), 85.
2. James Legge, *The Notions of the Chinese Concerning God and Spirits* (Hong Kong: Hong Kong Register Office, 1852), 99.
3. Winfried Corduan, *Neighboring Faiths: A Christian introduction to world religions* (Downers Grove, IL: InterVarsity Press, 1998), 136.

4   Benjamin I. Schwartz, *The World of Thought in Ancient China* (Cambridge, MA: Belknap Press, 1985), 21.

5   Winfried Corduan, *In The Beginning God: A fresh look at the case for original monotheism* (Nashville, TN: Broadman & Holman, 2013), 332.

6   See Legge, *The Notions of the Chinese*.

7   Schwartz, 30.

8   See Corduan, *In The Beginning God*, for a detailed apologetics for this.

9   Michael Molloy, *Experiencing The World's Religions: Tradition, challenge, and change*, 4th ed. (New York, NY: McGraw Hill, 2008), 218.

10 Kwan Kai Man and Han Siyi, "The Search For God in Chinese Culture and Contemporary China," *Canadian Social Science*, 4.3 (June 2008), 27–41.

11 Corduan, *Neighboring Faiths*, 285.

12 Geoffrey Parrinder, *The World's Living Religions* (London, UK: Pan Books Ltd.,1964), 97.

13 Corduan, *Neighboring Faiths*, 286.

14 Schwartz, 192.

15 H.G. Creel, *Chinese Thought from Confucius to Mao Tse-tung* (London, UK: Methuen, 1962), 110.

16 Robert Cummings Neville, *Ritual and Deference: Extending Chinese philosophy in a comparative context* (Albany, NY: State University of New York, 2008), 43.

17 Creel, 110.

18 Creel, 110.

19 Creel, 109.

20 Creel, 111.

21 Thomas Cleary, *Vitality, Energy, Spirit: A Taoist sourcebook* (Boston, MA: Shambhala, 1991), 7.

22 Julia Ching and Hans Kung, *Christianity and Chinese Religions* (New York, NY: Doubleday, 1989), 131

23 Ching and Kung, 131.

24 Creel, 113.

25 Parrinder, 100.

26 Creel, 113.

27 Creel, 122.

28 Corduan, *Neighboring Faiths*, 287.

29 Creel, 112.

30 Creel, 112–3.

31 Parrinder, 98.

32 Corduan, *Neighboring Faiths*, 288.

33 Creel, 114.

34 Creel, 121.

35 Creel, 121.

36 Molloy, 229–30.

37 Creel, 112.

38 Molloy, 231.

39 Parrinder, 91.

Chapter 4

1   H.G. Creel, *Chinese Thought from Confucius to Mao Tse-tung* (Chicago, IL: Mentor, 1963),

40.

2 Creel, 29.

3 Creel, 43.

4 Tong Zhang and Barry Schwartz, "Confucius and the Cultural Revolution: A Study in Collective Memory," *International Journal of Politics, Culture and Society*, 11.2 (1997): 193.

5 Julia Ching and Hans Kung, *Christianity and Chinese Religions* (New York, NY: Doubleday, 1989), 67.

6 Geoffrey Parrinder, *The World's Living Religions* (London, UK: Pan, 1964), 91.

7 Yao XinZhong, *An introduction to Confucianism* (Cambridge, UK: Cambridge University Press, 2000), 17.

8 Michael Molloy, *Experiencing The World's Religions: Tradition, challenge, and change*, 4th ed. (New York, NY: McGraw Hill, 2008), 239.

9 They will be introduced only briefly here as we will explore them in greater detail in the following chapter.

10 Michael Brannigan, *The Pulse of Wisdom: The Philosophies of India, China and Japan*, 2nd ed. (Belmont, CA: Wadsworth, 2000), 26.

11 Parrinder, 94.

12 Brannigan, 26.

13 Brannigan, 27.

14 James Legge, trans., *The Chinese Classics, Vol. II*, rev. 2nd ed. (Oxford, UK: Clarendon, 1895), 81.

15 Winfried Corduan, *Neighboring Faiths: A Christian Introduction to World Religions* (Downers Grove, IL: InterVarsity Press, 1998), 293.

16 The Confucian Golden Rule is sometimes referred to as the Silver Rule as it is the negative form of the more common Golden Rule.

17 Daniel A. Bell, the controversial political theorist, is one of the strongest proponents of this model. Read more about his arguments in *The China Model: Political Meritocracy and the Limits of Democracy* (Princeton, NJ: Princeton University Press, 2015).

Chapter 5

1 Geoffrey Parrinder, *The World's Living Religions* (London, UK: Pan, 1964), 105.

2 Peter J. Leihart, "When East is West," *First Things*, May 2005, https://www.firstthings.com/article/2005/05/when-east-is-west, accessed 11 October 2016.

3 His Holiness The XIVth Dalai Lama, "Religious Harmony and The Bodhgaya Interviews," in *Christianity Through Non-Christian Eyes*, ed. Paul J. Griffiths (Maryknoll, NY: Orbis Books, 1990), 169. (as quoted in Yandell, 109).

4 Elizabeth J. Harris, *What Buddhists Believe* (Oxford, UK: Oneworld, 1998), 12.

5 Harold Netland and Keith Yandell, *Buddhism: a Christian exploration and appraisal* (Downers Grove, IL: InterVarsity Press, 2009), 11.

6 Netland and Yandell, 13.

7 Molloy, 130.

8 Netland and Yandell, 19.

9 Netland and Yandell, 19.

10 This idea of no-self especially differentiates Buddhist thought from Hindu thought. Hindus believe in an eternal soul while the Buddhists claim that the notion of an individual soul is merely an illusion.

11 Netland and Yandell, 20.

12 The Samyutta-nikaya, v.420, as quoted by Sarvepalli Radhakrishnan and Charles A.

Moore, eds., "Buddhism," in *A Source Book in Indian Philosophy* (Bombay, MH: Oxford University Press, 1957), 274–5.

[13] Netland and Yandell, 17.

[14] Parrinder, 102–3.

[15] H.G. Creel, *Chinese Thought from Confucius to Mao Tse-tung* (Chicago, IL: Mentor, 1963), 153.

[16] Parrinder, 105.

[17] Creel, 161.

[18] Miikka Ruokanen and Paulos Huang, eds., *Christianity and Chinese Culture* (Grand Rapids, MI: Eerdmans, 2010), 90.

[19] Creel, 161.

[20] Creel, 160.

[21] Ch'u Chai and Winberg Chai, *Confucianism* (Hauppauge, NY: Barron's Educational Series, 1973), 112.

[22] Chai and Chai, 112.

[23] Chai and Chai, 113.

[24] Read more about Tu WeiMing's project in "Confucianism" in Robert C. Neville, *Ritual and Deference: Extending Chinese Philosophy in a Comparative Context* (Albany, NY: State University of New York Press: 2008), 66–69.

[25] Tu WeiMing, "The Meaning of Life: The Big Picture," *Life Magazine*, December 1988 as quoted at http://www.maryellenmark.com/text/magazines/life/905W-000-037.html, accessed August 5, 2017.

Chapter 6

[1] Yao XinZhong, *An Introduction to Confucianism* (Cambridge, UK: Cambridge University Press, 2000), 22.

[2] Yao, 22.

[3] Yao, 22.

[4] Yao, 26.

[5] Michael C. Brannigan, *The Pulse of Wisdom: The philosophies of India, China, and Japan*, 2nd ed. (Belmont, CA: Wadsworth, 2000), 25.

[6] Ching and Kung, 74.

[7] H.G. Creel, *Confucius and the Chinese Way* (New York, NY: Harper Torchbooks, 1960), 47.

[8] Julia Ching and Hans Kung, *Christianity and Chinese Religions* (New York, NY: Doubleday and Collins, 1989), 74.

[9] Creel, 44.

[10] Creel, 51.

[11] Ching and Kung, 109.

[12] Miikka Ruokanen and Paulos Huang, eds., *Christianity and Chinese Culture* (Grand Rapids, MI: Eerdmans, 2010), 34.

[13] Ruokanen and Huang, 80.

[14] Ching and Kung, 72.

[15] Ching and Kung, 73.

[16] Ching and Kung, 322.

[17] Brannigan, 25.

[18] Creel, 229.

[19] Bryan W. Van Norden, "Mencius and Augustine on Evil: A Test Case for Compara-

tive Philosophy," in *Roads to Wisdom: Chinese and Analytic Philosophical Traditions*, ed. Bo Mou (Peru, IL: Carus, 2001), 327.

[20] Van Norden, 328.

[21] Ching and Kung, 71.

[22] Creel, 230.

[23] Ching and Kung, 74.

[24] H.G. Creel, *Chinese Thought from Confucius to Mao Tse-tung* (London, UK: Methuen, 1962), 45.

[25] Ching and Kung, 88.

[26] Creel, *Confucius and the Chinese Way*, 51.

[27] Brannigan, 25.

[28] Brannigan, 25.

[29] Ching and Kung, 90.

[30] Ching and Kung, 68.

[31] Ching and Kung, 69.

[32] Ching and Kung, 69.

Chapter 7

[1] Cornelius Plantinga, Jr., *Not The Way It's Supposed To Be: A breviary of sin* (Grand Rapids, MI: Eerdmans, 1995), 1.

[2] Plantinga, 2.

[3] Plantinga, 11.

[4] Plantinga, 8.

[5] Plantinga, 10.

[6] Plantinga, 14.

[7] Albert H. Baylis, *From Creation To The Cross* (Grand Rapids, MI: Zondervan, 1996), 31.

[8] Paul G. Hiebert, *Anthropological Reflections on Missiological Issues* (Grand Rapids, MI: Baker, 1994), 210.

[9] Nicholas Wolterstorff, *Until Justice and Peace Embrace* (Grand Rapids, MI: Eerdmans, 1983) 70.

[10] Wolterstorff, 69.

[11] Plantinga, 9.

[12] Wolterstorff, 69.

[13] Wolterstorff, 70.

[14] Wolterstorff, 124.

[15] Walter Brueggemann, *Living Toward A Vision: Biblical Reflections on Shalom* (Philadelphia, PA: United Church Press, 1976), 16–17.

[16] Hiebert, 212.

[17] Brueggemann, 20.

[18] Brueggemann, 16.

Chapter 8

[1] Liu Xiaobo, *Ming Pao Monthly*, August 1989, 36. Quoted in Julia Ching, *Probing China's Soul: Religion, Politics, and Protest in the People's Republic* (New York, NY: Harper & Row, 1990), 141.

[2] http://www.scmp.com/news/china/society/article/2097437/outcry-after-chinese-woman-hit-car-ignored-run-over-again, accessed October 5, 2017.

[3] https://en.wikipedia.org/wiki/2008_Chinese_milk_scandal, accessed October 5, 2017.

4   Yu Hua, transl. Allan H. Barr, *China in Ten Words*, (London, UK: Duckworth Overlook, 2013), 25.

5   Yu, 25.

6   https://www.chinasource.org/resource-library/chinese-church-voices/why-china-needs-a-higher-righteousness, accessed October 6, 2017.

7   Romans 7:15–16.

8   Miikka Ruokanen and Paulos Huang, eds., *Christianity and Chinese Culture* (Grand Rapids, MI: Eerdmans, 2010), 34.

9   H.G. Creel, *Chinese Thought from Confucius to Mao Tse-tung* (London, UK: Methuen, 1962), 52.

10 Creel, 50.

11 Ruokanen and Huang, 8.

12 https://www.economist.com/news/china/21582295-soul-searching-debate-rages-about-apathy-towards-those-need-unkindness-strangers, accessed October 5, 2017.

13 James Legge, *Chinese Classics*, Vol. 2 (Oxford, UK: Clarendon Press, 1895), 26.

14 Ruokanen and Huang, 9.

15 Paul Hiebert, *Anthropological Reflections on Missiological Issues* (Grand Rapids, MI: Baker, 1994), 86.

16 Boye Lafayette De Menthe, *The Chinese Mind* (North Clarendon, VT: Tuttle, 2009).

17 Creel, 23.

18 Michael C. Brannigan, *The Pulse of Wisdom: The philosophies of India, China, and Japan*, 2nd ed. (Belmont, CA: Wadsworth, 2000), 23.

19 Brannigan, 25.

20 Brannigan, 24.

21 Simon Chan, *Grassroot Asian Theology: Thinking the Faith From the Ground Up* (Downers Grove, IL: IVP Academic, 2014), 38.

22 De Menthe, 11.

23 Creel, *Chinese Thought*, 13.

24 Creel, *Chinese Thought*, 12.

25 George A. Hood, *Neither Bang Nor Whimper: The end of a missionary era in China* (Singapore: Presbyterian Church, 1991), 1.

26 Hood, 1.

27 Hood, 2.

28 De Menthe, 173.

29 Chicken essence is a popular Chinese health tonic believed to promote general health and increase mental stamina. It is basically a distillation of chicken broth.

30 Winfried Corduan, http://wincorduan.bravejournal.com/entry/54392, accessed June, 12, 2017.

31 Ruokanen and Huang, 277.

32 Ruokanen and Huang, 277.

33 Chan, 34.

34 The book of Ruth tells the story of a kinsman-redeemer where Boaz is the kinsman-redeemer of Naomi and Ruth. In the story, Boaz modeled the type of true fasting that the prophet Isaiah had called Israel to observe (Isa. 58:7) — sharing food with the hungry and helping relatives in their time of need. The idea of helping or caring for our family members and relatives is therefore not one that is alien to the biblical worldview but one that is advocated as "true fasting".

35 Han Junxue, *Jidujiao yu Yunnan shaoshu minzu* (Kunming, YN: Yunnan Renmin, 2000),

178, as quoted in Ruokanen and Huang, eds., 177.

[36] Douglas J. Moo, *The Epistle to the Romans* (Grand Rapids, MI: Eerdmans, 1996), 148–157.

[37] Walter Brueggemann, *Living Toward a Vision: Biblical Reflections on Shalom* (Philadelphia, PA: United Church Press, 1976), 15.

[38] Brueggemann, 15.

[39] Brueggemann, 16.

[40] Jiang Menglin as quoted by Chen YongTao, "The Sinicization of Christinity: A Chinese Christian's Thoughts." *Chinese Theological Review*, 27 (2015): 142.

[41] Yao XinZhong, *An Introduction to Confucianism* (Cambridge, UK: Cambridge University Press, 2000), 75–76.

[42] James Legge, *The Works of Mencius* (Oxford, UK: Clarendon, 1895; reprint, New York, NY: Dover, 1970), 447.

[43] Yao, 76.

[44] Yao, 78.

[45] Brueggemann, 44.

[46] Barry Webb, *The Message of Isaiah: On eagle's wings* (Leicester, UK: InterVarsity Press, 1996), 170.

[47] Webb, 171.

[48] Julia Ching, *Mysticism and Kingship in China: The heart of Chinese wisdom* (Cambridge, UK: Cambridge University Press, 1997), 36.

[49] *Shangdi* is the title that is used to refer to the Supreme Lord or literally, Lord of Heaven.

[50] Enoch Wan, "Practical contextualization: A case study of evangelizing contemporary Chinese," *Chinese Around the World* (March 2000): 18–24.

[51] Jackson Wu's book, *Saving God's Face: A Chinese Contextualization of Salvation through Honor and Shame* (Pasadena, CA: WCIU Press, 2012) is an excellent resource on the discussion of the Cultural Chinese's concept of face in the context of the Gospel.

[52] Ruokanen and Huang, 70.

GRACEW♥RKS

Graceworks is a publishing and training consultancy based in Singapore, dedicated to promoting spiritual friendship in church and society, and seeing lives transformed through books that present truth for life.

Our desire is for our publications to help people apply biblical truths to the challenges of daily living, enabling them to live as genuine disciples of Christ in our complex and challenging world. We have a particular passion to nurture and publish local Singaporean and Southeast Asian authors.

Our publications can be found on our online store, *www.graceworks.com.sg*. Paperbacks are also available on Bookdepository and Amazon and eBooks on Kindle, iBooks , Google Play and Kobo.

You can contact us at *enquiries@graceworks.com.sg*, or follow us on Facebook (@GraceworksSG) and Instagram (graceworkssg).